THE BOOK OF REVELATION

A Catholic Interpretation of the Apocalypse

Reverend John Tickle

LIGUORI
PUBLICATIONS

One Liguori Drive
Liguori, Missouri 63057
(314) 464-2500

Imprimi Potest:
John F. Dowd, C.SS.R.
Provincial, St. Louis Province
The Redemptorists

Imprimatur:
Monsignor Edward J. O'Donnell
Vicar General, Archdiocese of St. Louis

ISBN 0-89243-195-4
Library of Congress Catalog Card Number: 83-82062

Cover design and interior artwork by Pam Hummelsheim

The cover photo, by Leonard Von Matt, shows the dome mosaic in
the Galla Placidia Mausoleum in Ravenna, Italy. In the center of
the dome is the "unconquered cross" radiating in every direction.
At the corners the four creatures, symbolizing the four evangelists,
suggest the spreading of Christ's Gospel to the four corners of the
earth (see Revelation 4:7).

Table of Contents

PART THREE
The Church Transfigured (Revelation 21, 22)
Of the New Jerusalem

Preface

Let me share with you how this text on the Catholic interpretation of the Book of Revelation came about.

I love the Scriptures of the Lord and what they reveal to me and to all of us each day; so I never tire in sharing with others what I know about this wonderful font of inspiration. In no way am I a scholar of the Scriptures, but I thank the good Lord for those he has called to be scholars. I also thank him for letting me pastor a parish community of two thousand families — even though at times I really become exhausted. Our Scriptures originated in the *living* community of the people of Old Testament times and the disciples of the early Christian community. Much of what I write about our Scriptures comes from my deep and loving personal reflection on the *living* experience of our parish community.

In the fall of 1982 a number of parishioners asked me if I would deliver a series of evening lectures on the Catholic interpretation of the Book of Revelation. Over three hundred people came to study and pray together during this series. We taped the lectures, and then my good friend Kathy Black dedicatedly transcribed the tapes into written form. With the same devotion, another good friend, Doris King, edited the copy from the written/spoken form into "book" form. It was a monumental task, but it accomplished what we had hoped for — most of the free style of the spoken word was retained in written form. Several editings later, the final version was arrived at. My eternal thanks to these two dedicated servants of our community.

Our hope and prayer is that all who read this and study the beautiful message of REVELATION will be deeply touched by the Spirit and the consoling message that Jesus is Lord forever and ever and we are united with him unto glory.

Father John Tickle, Rector
Immaculate Heart of Mary Cathedral
Las Cruces, New Mexico

Introduction

The study of the Book of Revelation brings us into intimate contact with our risen Lord: our Savior, the Master of the universe, the Lord of creation, the Power by which we live each day, realizing the fullness of what it is to be alive. It brings us John — the one to whom our Lord revealed himself — with a Revelation meant for all times. Through this Book we begin to see God's power and glory in every moment of history; we begin to understand that no matter what we do as his sons and daughters, no matter what we are, *he* is the Victor, the Lord of the universe; and we begin to realize that all things will be as he promised, lifted up through his Passion and Resurrection and exaltation to glory and power.

As we study together, may the Lord teach us how to be one with him so that we may share his message and bring his love, his compassion, and his understanding to our times.

We are co-creators with him in the ''new world'' that he wishes ours to be. May he use us as he will, in order that we may bring his revelation to the fullness of life to ourselves and to all around us.

To him be praise and glory forever and ever. Amen.

Before we begin, however, let me share with you my own feelings about the "neoapocalyptic" authors whose books are to be found almost everywhere, the new-day prophets of doom, warning us of disaster that will take place at a certain time. Let us suppose, for instance, that total disaster is to take place at 7:23 P.M. on a given day. When that moment arrives, if they are wrong in their prediction, we will survive. But, if they are right, we will have had it; that's all there is to it. Now there is a very solid 2,000-year tradition of the Catholic Church concerning the Book of Revelation. Yet, certain modern authors persist in propagating theories that not only confuse and cause a deep consternation within the hearts and minds of their readers but also promulgate a misunderstanding about Jesus Christ as he is portrayed in the Book of Revelation. It's time for those of us who believe this teaching of 2,000 years to share what our tradition has revealed to us about this particular Book of the New Testament.

Our presentation does not constitute a polemic, nor is it an attempt to refute the statements of the "neo-apocalyptics." It is simply an introduction to the interpretation of the Roman Catholic Church in regard to the symbols, message, and theme of the Book of Revelation. It is important for us, as Christians in the Catholic tradition, to know in detail what the teaching of our tradition is in regard to this very special, very beautiful, ecstasy-evoking Book of Revelation.

Chapter 1
Background and Theme of Revelation

I remember my mother telling me, when I was a young boy, about the doomsday prophets of her own childhood. This was in the early 1900s, when she was a young girl in grade school under the tutelage of the Sisters. There was one nun who always impressed her as being the font of all knowledge. So, my mother went up to her, very scared after hearing all this apocalyptic doom, and asked: "Sister, when will the world come to an end?" Sister looked at her and replied: "When you die, and then you'll know."

There is a particular passage from Scripture which nullifies all the predictions of the prophets of doom. In the Gospel of Saint Matthew, Jesus — in answer to a question about the end of the world — says: "As for the exact day or hour, no one knows it, neither the angels in heaven nor the Son, but the Father only." And in verse 42 he reminds his followers: "Stay awake, therefore! You cannot know the day your Lord is coming." (See Matthew 24:36,42.)

"The day that your Lord is coming" is the day of the end of the world. If, then, "We cannot know the day the Lord is coming," we cannot know the day of the end of the world.

In the Second Letter of Peter, there is another passage that should be considered before we begin our interpretation of the Book of Revelation. It deals with a problem that Christianity has had to cope with from the beginning. Peter had been chosen by the Lord to be the leader of the Church; he gave him the keys to the Kingdom. And the author of Peter's Letters — referring to the Letters of Paul — says: "There are certain passages in them hard to understand. The ignorant and the unstable distort them (just as they do the rest of Scripture) to their own ruin" (2 Peter 3:16). We often hear predictions of those who claim that they can interpret the Scriptures by looking at our modern situation while taking out of context what they read in the Book of Revelation. This passage from Peter should warn us all to be careful.

With this thought in mind we begin our study of Revelation by examining the backdrop, the background of the Book itself.

All Scripture emerges from a living background. There is a political and a social living reality in which God reveals himself. The Lord's revelation comes to people as they exist in a given culture. They sense that it is the Lord speaking to them. This has always been the Lord's way — from the beginning of time. He reveals himself to his people in the place and time in which they are.

To fully appreciate this Book, we have to understand what was going on in the first century following the death of Jesus; only then can Revelation be understood in our own time. We have to know *the context in which this book was put together, talked about, shared, and eventually written down.*

So, what were the political and social conditions of that first century when this Book of Revelation was written? And what are its theological and ethical themes?

Political and Social Environment

The first century after the death of Christ was a time of persecution for the early Christian community. These men and women were living under tremendous tension. They had this deep conviction that Jesus, who had been born in Bethlehem, had suffered and died, and had risen from the dead, was with them in the Spirit. This basic message of the apostles is called the "kerygma." And their followers in that first century proclaimed that Jesus, who had been crucified, had risen and would return again at the end of time. That same message is repeated at Mass today when we proclaim: "Christ has died, Christ is risen, Christ will come again."

The early Christians were convinced that Jesus had saved them and that they would be victorious. He had suffered a horrible death on a cross. But he had risen from the dead and was with them through the power of the Spirit, and they felt that power in their lives.

Now — perhaps because of this intense conviction — there began a series of unbelievable persecutions. As Christians, day in and day out they had to face the reality of tremendous negative experiences: persecution, even to the point of execution. Because of their belief, thousands of individual Christians — sometimes entire Christian communities — were martyred for their faith. Much like their Jewish ancestors, who never doubted that Yahweh — the name that the Jews gave to God — was with them and protecting them, they suffered persecution from one generation to the next.

This conviction of our early Christian ancestors is echoed in modern Catholic life. We face difficulties every day; yet, deep down inside of us, we say, "I don't know what I'd do if it weren't for my faith. If Jesus isn't winning, then I'm losing. That's all there is to it. I don't know how I'd get by every day except for the strength and power that the Lord

11

gives me." However, what we have to face differs from the early-Christian type of persecution. To be a Christian in America is relatively easy. Oh, we may be laughed at, and people may think we're stupid; but we can disregard these things because we live in a milieu in which being a Christian is possible. We don't have to fight against a massive system which not only does not believe in one God but also worships countless pagan gods. The early Christian community — and this was also true of their Jewish ancestors — was tempted very often to compromise with the pagan customs around them, to give in a little bit to them, to coexist with paganism.

It was under these circumstances that the Book of Revelation was written: Christians were convinced that Jesus had won the victory, through his Resurrection, over all sin and over all evil; but those same Christians had to live in a society which persecuted them for their convictions. No doubt, they were tempted to say, "Well, if he's won already and we're redeemed, then maybe we can give in a little bit and compromise with this society. What difference will it make?" In a way, this same temptation can be just as enticing to us when we are faced with the materialistic and secularistic "values" of our society today.

The Book of Revelation, however, will say: "Compromise in any of the teachings and the value system of Jesus Christ is *out of the question* for the followers of Jesus Christ." That is its basic message.

Now, how did these persecutions come about? They were instigated by the Roman emperors who reigned in the first century following the death of Christ. They began with the cruel and depraved Nero, who blamed the burning of Rome on the Christians. Nero insanely declared that he was "God." And he acted like it. He ruled the world. There began with Nero what became known as the "imperial cult." He had himself proclaimed "divine." Each successive emperor then proclaimed that *he* was "divine"; and they had temples built across the Roman Empire for the honor and worship of themselves.

This was bad news for the Jewish people — both those who retained their ancient faith and those who had begun to follow Jesus. Both of these groups were in a quandary. If Nero was the best that could be offered, why worship at all? It wasn't worth the struggle. The emperor had imperial authority; he had armies; he had the power to tax; and he could persecute to death those who did *not* worship him. This is the atmosphere in which the early Christian communities found themselves.

However, it should be noted that when Rome conquered a nation it had a very clever way of ruling these newly acquired lands. This astuteness is one of the reasons why the Romans were able to increase the empire to the extent that they did. Furthermore, it enabled them to rule diverse and large numbers of people. They allowed the local populace to retain its own culture as long as the people paid taxes to the emperors. And, in the case of the Jews, Rome allowed them — by law — to worship their God.

The Jewish people therefore had the right, under Roman law, to worship as Jews. (Only under the Emperor Caligula — for a short period of time — was this exemption ignored.) If they could show that they were still practicing their ancient religious rites, they could not be forced to participate in the imperial cult inaugurated by Nero and succeeding emperors.

To understand what happened next we should recall what is recorded in the Acts of the Apostles. Those Jews who believed in Jesus — the apostles and their many followers — never quite broke with their Jewish tradition. They would go to the temple and would participate in the temple worship. Then they would retire into their homes to eat the Paschal meal, to celebrate the Eucharist. They more or less kept one foot in Judaism and one foot in the New Judaism, the fulfillment of Judaism. They never considered renouncing their Jewish ancestry because they were following the Jew from Nazareth.

Now the non-Christian Jews continued to worship in their temples — particularly in certain cities to which these first letters in the Book of Revelation are addressed. If they could show that they were not "tainted" with Christianity, they were allowed to worship in peace. To prove this to the Roman authorities they began to exclude the Jewish Christians from their temple worship.

So the early Christian community finds itself under fire from two fronts. They are being persecuted by the Roman authorities who are trying to force them to worship the emperor, and they are being persecuted by the non-Christian Jews. It is out of this social milieu and from this political background that the Book of Revelation evolves. It views imperial Rome and strict Judaism as being exploitive, destructive, and dehumanizing of the Body of Christ.

Theological Theme

The theological theme of Revelation is made manifest in this conflict between pagan Rome and the Christian community.

Rome says, "We're the greatest." The emperor says, "Build a temple and worship me. I am the power of the world. I am the power of the universe. Rome is the justice of the universe; Rome is the power of the universe. Without Rome, there is no universe." Rome spells it out very clearly. "If you don't agree with this, you will die." (And this was especially true during the reign of the Emperor Domitian. Thousands died because they did not accept pagan Rome's point of view.)

Christianity says — in the Book of Revelation — that power and justice belong to Jesus Christ, not Rome. The only power and the only justice in the universe lie in the risen Lord. They do not rest with any group of men or with any government. Jesus is Leader. He has conquered; he is conquering; and he will continue to conquer. Not Caesar but Jesus Christ is Victor. That is the theological theme of this Book. Against that theme we can judge all our values; we can judge the values of all nations; we can judge the values of all communities of people. "JESUS CHRIST IS VICTOR."

The entire Book of Revelation elaborates on this theme — spelling out what it means to the individual, to the local community, to the governments of the world, to the world itself. The risen Christ is Victor. The entire world belongs to him for all eternity.

Ethical Theme

Now, what is the ethical theme, the moral point of view, emphasized in the Book of Revelation? This Book — addressed to the early Christian community and to us today — summons us to stamp out evil in our own community and to personally commit ourselves to wipe out all evil, never compromising with it. We must practice loyal resistance — through the power of our risen Lord — to the unchristian values which surround us on every side. *There is no room for compromise!* This calls for a moral commitment to resist evil.

The Book of Revelation exhorts the faithful to loyally resist any temptation to compromise with the world and its pagan values. It also spells out the censures reserved for those who fail in this regard.

One of the key passages in Revelation is contained in chapter 11, verse 15: "Then the seventh angel blew his trumpet. Loud voices in heaven cried out, 'The kingdom of the world now belongs to our Lord and to his Anointed One, and he shall reign forever and ever.' " Jesus is Lord of the universe. And, if we want to follow the ethical theme described above, we must keep that in mind.

So, the Book of Revelation is calling the entire world,

Christian and non-Christian, to repentance and commitment. Jesus is not just the Lord of the Christian world. He is Lord over the *entire* universe. He is calling all people to repentance and to faithful resistance to pagan influences and values.

Now, although Revelation is meant for all people in general, we should not lose sight of the fact that it speaks to each one of us individually. But note that our purpose here is not just to calculate numbers and figure out who is 666. Nor is it our main concern to find out who is the anti-Christ, whether Russia is this or that, and whether this or that passage refers to certain individuals. No, we will deal with the basic message of Apocalypse now. Revelation insists that we resist worldwide pagan influences and unchristian attitudes in our own relationships — between wives and husbands, parents and children, ourselves and others. If our present-day values do not match the value system of Jesus Christ, the Book of Revelation reminds us to resist them — both as individuals and as a community.

The Book of Revelation begins with letters to the seven churches of the Asian area. As we travel from city to city, we may just find ourselves living in one or the other of them. Their "neighborhood" may be similar to our neighborhood, their household like our household. And we will be called upon to resist, even as the early Christians were called to resist.

Review and Discussion

1. How did the "kerygma" of the apostles sustain the Christian communities during their persecution?
2. Check the correct answer to this question: What was the greatest temptation for the early Christians?
   1) To hide and practice their religion in secret.
   2) To compromise with pagan values and customs around them.
   3) To attempt to conquer all unbelievers with force.

3. Check the correct answer to this statement: Christians were persecuted by the Roman Empire because:
   1) Rome was afraid that the Christians might revolt.
   2) Christians would not worship the emperor.
   3) Rome was trying to destroy Palestine.
4. Why did some of the Jewish leadership also begin to persecute Christians?
5. Summarize in your own words the political/social environment surrounding the early Church.
6. According to the Book of Revelation — in contradiction to the Roman point of view — all power and justice belong to _____ .
7. The Book of Revelation calls the entire world to _____ and _____ .
8. What is the ethical theme of this Book?
9. In what areas of your life do you let the Lord Jesus reign?
10. In what areas of your life do you keep him from having influence?

Moment of Prayerful Reflection

1. Read Revelation 11:15.
2. Meditate on what this passage tells you about the Lord Jesus and what that means in your life.

Let Us Pray

Lord Jesus, it fills us with such strength, power, and comfort to rest our lives in your glory and power. May we be inspired each day to turn our lives, with all our problems and difficulties, over to you. Then, animated with your powerful Spirit, we pray to have the courage to resist evil and to actively promote the values of your Kingdom. We give you praise, honor, and love, for you are our Lord forever and ever. Come, Lord Jesus. Amen.

Chapter 2
Authorship and Style of the Book

Authorship

Was John the Apostle the actual author of Revelation? This has been a matter of considerable controversy among biblical scholars for centuries. Much of the imagery — *Lamb of God*, for example — is reminiscent of the Gospel of John. But a problem arises from the fact that John's Gospel is written in beautiful Greek; whereas Revelation is composed by a scholar poor in Greek — someone who knew Aramaic and translated into Greek and poorly at that.

The authorship of the fourth Gospel and the Book of Revelation remains unsettled. True, both works bear the name John, but they were probably written by his "spiritual children," with John being the main oral source. This would account for both the similarities of thought and usage, as well as the differences in language. Also, it was customary in those days to attribute a work to an author even though he did not do the actual writing.

Regardless of who did the actual writing of Revelation, it is certain that this person (or persons) was thoroughly acquainted with Old Testament writings, especially the Books of Exodus, Daniel, and Psalms, as well as the prophets Ezekiel, Isaiah, and Zechariah. This is evident from the symbols and images taken from the Old Testament and used in Revelation.

Style

As to the style of writing, the author of the Book of Revelation used the "apocalyptic" approach. We might compare apocalyptic literature to the works of science fiction writers, who project a future scientific world based on what they know of science past and science present.

This style of writing apocalyptically was prevalent during a short span of Jewish history. Authors began to write apocalyptically some two hundred years before Jesus, and this style prevailed until some two hundred years after the death of Jesus. It has very specific characteristics.

Apocalyptic writers take the past, the present, and the future and mingle them all together. Hence it is almost impossible to discern when they are talking about the past or when they are talking about the present. Once this has been done, they use cryptic symbols to concoct images that reflect this combined perspective. Next, they look to the future and predict it, based on past and present experiences. (In the Book of Revelation those experiences are the sufferings of the early Christian community.) They say: "Here we are, and this is how we're suffering, and this is what's going on, and these are the promises of the Lord to us during his life; therefore, this shall take place in the future."

It is important to understand the difference between prophecy and apocalypse, because all doomsday writers nowadays claim Revelation is prophetic. But the Book is not prophetic in the sense that they claim.

What do we mean by *prophecy?* To a certain extent, all of us are "prophets." My mother, for instance, was a great prophet. We had friends in a neighboring city whom we visited with great regularity. My behavior at that time had been causing my parents quite a problem. Each time we drove to visit our friends we passed through an area where there was a prison. It was then that my mother would turn to me and open her mouth in prophecy. She would say, in no uncertain terms: "At the rate you're going, there is your home."

The prophets looked at how the community was living at that moment and compared it with how the community was *supposed* to be living, based on God's word as revealed by the prophets and the patriarchs. Next, they said to the people: "This is what the Lord says will happen!" The prophets repeat this formula time and again: "This is what the Lord says is to be done. This is what you are doing. Therefore, this is what is going to happen to you." Then, based on the actions of the people judged against what they were supposed to be doing, the prophets would make their prediction about the future.

That is what prophecy is. It says to the people: "Watch out, you're slipping. Remember the past." By its very nature, then, prophecy involves hope: hope that the people will shape up, that they will get the message and make the proper changes. All the prophets had a deep sense of hope. They were frustrated, time after time after time; but they had hope!

What is meant by *apocalypse?* Apocalyptic writing is a form of prophecy insofar as the same reflection takes place. The Book of Revelation is prophetic in this sense: "Here's what Jesus promised, this is what you are doing, and this is what will result." Prophecy ends on a note of hope: "Just get with the program and change your heart, convert and go back to what the covenant demands. Go back to God and do what he says, and this bleak future will not happen." But apocalypse — especially *the* Apocalypse — by stressing death and destruction appears to eliminate hope. Modern doomsday writers have concentrated on this one aspect of Revelation, and what they are saying is this: "You're doomed. There is no hope for you or me to try to do anything." So, prophecy says: "There's hope that I can do it, that the community can do it, that the Church can do it, that we can get together and change our ways and repent and move on." But Apocalypse — in the rhetoric of the doomsday writers — seems to be saying: "You don't have a chance."

Is there any way to change this gloomy apocalyptic attitude about salvation? Fortunately, there is — because Revelation concludes by saying: "Don't worry. Jesus has already done it. You didn't do it, and you weren't ever going to do it. So, *I'll* do it myself." Jesus Christ will bring us to fulfillment. We can't do it; but don't worry, because in the end he's going to win us over and win over everyone and everything.

This difference between prophecy and apocalypse is very important because of what all the modern doomsday writers are saying. They tell us that if we can get so-and-so to stop this and so-and-so to stop that everything will work out. For instance, if we can get the Russians to stop doing this and the Syrians to stop doing that, someone else to stop doing this and you and I to stop doing that, we can get it all together. That is the way they read the Book of Revelation.

This is in direct contrast to the Catholic interpretation of the Book of Revelation: Jesus Christ has redeemed the world. He is the glorified and exalted Son of Man who has conquered in the struggle between God and Satan. At the end of the world all powers hostile to God will be annihilated, and then will begin the everlasting Kingdom of God.

"But if I'm already saved," you may be thinking, "why should I worry? Why waste my time trying to be good if it doesn't make any difference anyway?" But the way you act does make a difference. This is the whole point of the Book of Revelation. Jesus is saying: "I have given you life; but if you want eternal life, you must respond to my love." (We cannot *feel* God's love until we react to it.)

Some years ago, while directing a catechetical program, I witnessed a scene that I will never forget. There was a special class for the hearing impaired. One of the little boys had misbehaved, and the teacher was bawling him out — shaking her finger at him. The boy just sat there; but, finally, he indicated he had had enough by walking to the center of the room and sitting down. He glanced at her and, then, covered his eyes. The look on the teacher's face was heartrending. She went to him and signed: "No, I love you. I'm sorry." But he had turned her off.

Isn't that exactly what we do? The Lord comes to us with his love and we just sit there. We turn him off not only with our eyes and ears but also with our minds and hearts. *We simply won't open up to his love*. We just sit there, closed up. Still he keeps *loving* us.

In order to present the revelation that Jesus is Victor, that he has won over evil for all time, the author of the Book of Revelation constructs a symbolic universe. He uses "Star-Wars" imagery with unbelievable, fantastic symbols, mainly taken from the Old Testament, and meshes them together in a seemingly illogical but dynamic way. And as these images spiral across the pages they resemble a fireworks display on the Fourth of July. Now, ordinarily, when we watch a display we don't sit there trying to explain what is happening. "What physical laws come into play here?" "That one has gone fifty feet; it should have six more bursts. . . ." We don't do that. Instead, we say, "Wow! Look at that one go!" Now, that's the Book of Revelation. It's an experience of watching the fireworks explode. There's no seeming logic to it. Of course, this fact poses a problem for us today when we try to understand the Book.

We in the Western World try to be so logical about everything.

But does everything have to be strictly logical? We read about an Oriental artist who sits down and spends five days staring at the rose he intends to paint. We think to ourselves: "That's not very productive. Hundreds more could have been painted if he had begun right away." But no, he has to contemplate it for five days before he paints it. And when the rose is finally painted, he tells us that *he* didn't paint the rose; the rose painted itself. And we say, "Oh, sure. Where's the general assembly line?"

We make this rude remark simply because we are very logically oriented. The Book of Revelation is not. It's a Fourth of July fireworks display. It's dynamic and spiraling. It's a symbolic universe in which the power and authority of Jesus Christ, as Victor, stand as a conquering power in spite of the community's suffering of poverty, persecution, and execution.

As we read the following chapters, I will be pointing out key symbols that appear in Revelation. Now that you understand the basic background of the Book, you will be better able to understand the imagery.

Review and Discussion

1. What are some of the characteristics of apocalyptic writing?
2. Check the correct answer in the following: Prophets were:
   1) soothsayers.
   2) fortune-tellers.
   3) men who proclaimed the future based on promises of the past and events of the present.
3. Is hope present in prophecy? in apocalyptic writing?
4. Revelation says the final outcome of the world depends on the power and victory of _____ .

5. Why should you try to respond to the way of the Lord according to Revelation?
6. Check the correct answer in the following: Revelation uses images and symbols to:
   1) describe the real world.
   2) present a logical explanation of the plan of God.
   3) inspire the followers of Jesus to emotionally experience his power and victory.

Moment of Prayerful Reflection

1. Read Revelation 15:3-4.
2. Meditate on how the Lord Jesus deserves your love, honor, and praise for all he has done for you!

Let Us Pray

Lord Jesus, bless us with your glorious power, that we may always shine forth to the world your love and peace. May all people come to know you and your way. May our worship and praise of your name bring grace and joy into all of creation. We offer you praise and honor forever. Come, Lord Jesus. Amen.

PART ONE

THE CHURCH INCARNATE

(Revelation 1-3)

OF SEVEN CHURCHES AND THEIR PROBLEMS

"Write down, therefore, whatever you see in visions. . . ."
(Revelation 1:19)

Chapter 3
Prelude to the Seven Letters
(Revelation 1)

As we begin our explanation and interpretation of Revelation we should keep in mind that the entire Book may be divided into three sections. In general, we will follow the divisions employed by Father Etienne Charpentier, in his book *How to Read the New Testament.* Part One is entitled "The Church Incarnate," consisting of chapters one through three; Part Two is entitled "The Church Committed," consisting of chapters four through twenty; and Part Three is entitled "The Church Transfigured," consisting of chapters twenty-one and twenty-two. This comprehensive view indicates that the entire Book is a kind of meditation on the Church.

The format of all seven letters found in the first three chapters of the Book is the same, even though they vary a bit. They don't all make the same points, but, basically, they have similar areas of interest. Each one begins with a command to write. John, the author, reports his "prophetic message" to "bear witness to the word of God and the testimony of Jesus Christ" who is "the One." Throughout the letters, the phrase "I know" personifies Jesus Christ. And what does he know? He describes the situation, and commends or censures his audience according to the circumstances. When necessary, he commands them to repent, and then reveals to them what is going to happen. And whenever he says that there will be a speedy coming of the Lord, it is important to place these words in the context of the times. (When the disciples heard Jesus say, "And know that I am with you always, until the end of the world" [Mark 28:20], they presumed that he was coming right away. They had no idea that it would be centuries later.)

All the letters end with an exhortation to hold fast, followed by a call to hear, to listen. This call goes out to all the churches and all the people. Each one finally concludes with a promise to those who will overcome and will stay steadfast and remain with the Lord.

Verses 1-3: "This is the revelation God gave to Jesus Christ, that he might show his servants what must happen very soon. He made it known by sending his angel to his servant John." So begins the Book of Revelation. Jesus is its source. The angel is the traditional messenger of God in apocalyptic literature. As a mark of respect, the Jews ordinarily did not pronounce the divine name. In the beginning they called him "Elohim." But God's name is "Yahweh," and only one person, once a year, was allowed to speak his name. That person was the high priest on the highest holy day, inside the sanctuary and inside the Holy of Holies. So, in the ancient literature of the Jews, angels were used to give the messages because God and his name were so holy. John uses this same form of imagery.

Verse 4: "To the seven churches in the province of Asia; John wishes you grace and peace — from him who is and who was and who is to come, and from the seven spirits before his throne." Seven is a symbolic number in the Book of Revelation. It, or any combination thereof, means fullness or completion. Sometimes the combination will be fours and threes, added together to make seven or multiplied to make twelve. So, wherever we see seven, four, three, or twelve we have a symbol for fullness and completion. It means the fullness of the Spirit of the Lord.

The seven churches to which these letters are addressed form almost a perfect circle in that part of the world which is now modern Turkey. John could have written to anybody under the sun. However, because geographically these cities form almost a perfect circle he uses that fact to symbolize that his message is to the universal Church.

Verses 5,6: Here we see the titles of Jesus: "the faithful witness, the first-born from the dead and ruler of the kings of earth." These titles together with the phrase "who loves us and freed us from our sins" speak of his Passion, Resurrection, and exaltation, which point to his rulership over the kings of the earth. Recall the purpose of Revelation: to remind the rulers of the earth that Jesus is Victor. So the Book begins by saying that Jesus — not Caesar — is ruler of the entire world.

Verses 7,8: "See, he comes amid the clouds" is a direct reference to Daniel 7:13. To come "amid the clouds" indicates the coming of the Messiah, the Judge of the world. "The Lord God says, 'I am the Alpha and the Omega.' " The first and last letters of the Greek alphabet — alpha and omega — are symbols of totality. Jesus is the beginning and the end.

Verses 9-16: After explaining how he came to the island of Patmos, from which he is writing, John describes his first vision. He sees "One like a Son of Man" and describes him somewhat like Daniel does in 7:9-15. His "robe" symbolizes priesthood; his "sash of gold," kingship; his "snow-white" hair, eternalness; "his eyes [blazing] like fire," infinite knowledge; "his feet . . . like polished brass," unchangeableness; "his voice . . . like the roar of rushing waters," divine authority. The "two-edged sword" refers to the word of God which will reward and punish on Judgment Day. And "his face [shining] like the sun at its brightest" indicates divine majesty.

Verses 17,18: "When I caught sight of him I fell down," as we all should in humility before the Lord. Then Jesus tells John: "There is nothing to fear. I am the First and the Last and the One who lives. . . . I hold the keys of death and the nether world." The word "keys" is a symbol. If we have the keys, we can get in and get out. We can lock in and we can lock out. We are masters of our houses because we have the keys. Jesus is Master of the universe because he has the keys.

Verses 19,20: "Write down, therefore, whatever you see in visions — what you see now and will see in time to come." This is a privilege of the prophets. The Lord gives them the power to perceive what is and what will come to be. Then, in the final verse of this chapter, he explains the secret meaning of the seven stars in his right hand and the seven lampstands of gold. "The seven stars are the presiding spirits [angels] of the seven churches, and the seven lampstands are the seven churches." The seven stars in his "right hand" are an allusion to contemporary imperial power — the emperors' crowns were decorated with the seven planets of the world, indicating that the emperors were the power of the universe. But Jesus has seven stars in his hand: He holds the fullness of authority over all the churches and fullness of protection over the Christian community. Truly he has the whole world in his hands.

Review and Discussion

1. In verse 1, the one who reveals is _____ .
2. At what time did the early Christians believe the world would come to an end?
3. Angels were the messengers of God in biblical literature because the Jews considered God _____ .
4. The number seven in Revelation is a symbol of _____
   _____ .

5. Verse 5 gives the titles of Jesus. They are:
   1) _____ .
   2) _____ .
   3) _____ .

6. Why does Revelation begin by saying that Jesus is the ruler of the kings of the earth?
7. What is the symbolic meaning of:
   1) "He comes amid the clouds" (verse 7)
   2) "His eyes blazed like fire" (verse 14)
   3) "His voice sounded like the roar of rushing waters" (verse 15)
   4) "A two-edged sword" (verse 16)
8. Why are seven churches addressed? What do they symbolize?
9. Jesus has seven stars in his right hand (verse 16). How does this allude to the Roman emperors?
10. Since Jesus holds the keys to death (verse 18), he is
    _____ .

11. What is the secret meaning of the seven stars and seven lampstands as explained in verse 20?
12. In your own life, list three ways in which the Lord reveals himself and his personal plan for you.
    1) _____ .
    2) _____ .
    3) _____ .

13. Why does the world look to its human rulers instead of to the Lord for guidance?

Moment of Prayerful Reflection

1. Read Revelation 1:1-3.
2. Meditate on your own personal relationship with the Lord Jesus and how carefully you listen to him and attempt to live his way.

Let Us Pray

Lord Jesus, you fill our hearts with joy and peace when we live your way of love, forgiveness, compassion, and acceptance of each other. Help us to make each day powerful in extending your Kingdom through our acts of love and kindness. May we be your witnesses to the ends of the earth. We give you our praise forever. Come, Lord Jesus. Amen.

Chapter 4
The First Four Letters
(Revelation 2)

In general, all seven of these letters to the churches in Asia Minor imply that the greatest danger to the early Christians was coming more from within than without. Some Christians were subscribing to the Gnostic theory on liberty, which freed them — they maintained — to participate in the imperial cult (in certain areas) and still remain Christians.

To Ephesus

The first letter is addressed to Ephesus, a city dedicated to the imperial cult, the worship of the emperor.

Verses 1-4: Jesus "walks among the seven lampstands of gold." This recalls the Lord God "moving about in the garden" as related in Genesis 3:8. As he walked God spoke intimately to Adam and Eve — and ultimately to us. Jesus commends the church for her "patient endurance" and for her courage in enduring hardships for his cause. But he is disappointed that they have turned aside from their "early love."

Verse 5: "Keep firmly in mind the heights from which you have fallen. Repent, and return to your former deeds. If you do not repent I will come to you and remove your lampstand [your church] from its place." *Repent and return to your former way of life*. These are the two stages of personal conversion. After first recalling what Jesus did for you, repent of what you did against him and, then, give witness to your Christianity before the world. That is full and total conversion. That is what Jesus is calling the churches to do. And that is what he is calling each one of us to do.

Verse 6: Here Jesus says: "You have this much in your favor: you detest the practices of the Nicolaitans, just as I do." The Nicolaitans were a secret cult of Christian impostors who said it was permissible to compromise with pagan practices. According to them, it was all right to eat the meat sacrificed to idols and to take part in the sexual excesses which were a part of the pagan religious observances. Nicolaitans maintained that they could still have Jesus Christ as their Lord even though they participated in these activities. But Jesus says no to all these practices.

Verse 7: "I will see to it that the victor eats from the tree of life which grows in the garden of God." This is a reference to Genesis 2:9 and, also, to the final chapter of Revelation. The tree of life which had been denied Adam is now accessible to his faithful ones who will conquer their own personal sins. They will have the tree of life, to live on its fruit and to have joy and happiness for all time.

To Smyrna

The next letter is addressed to Smyrna, a Jewish-dominated city north of Ephesus. It was extremely hostile to Christian Jews because the non-Christian Jews did not want to be associated with the followers of Jesus lest they, too, be persecuted by pagan Rome.

Verses 8,9: He "who once died but now lives" speaks to Smyrna's Christians as being poor and rich at the same time. "I know of your tribulation and your poverty, even though you are rich." They are poor because they are being persecuted, but they are rich because they have Jesus, the Victor.

Verse 10: "The devil will indeed cast some of you into prison to put you to the test; you will be tried over a period of ten days. Remain faithful until death and I will give you the crown of life." "Ten days" symbolizes a small amount of time. Ten days is nothing compared to an eternity of happiness. What will they receive for ten days of persecution? The "crown of life" which symbolizes victory and eternal glory.

Verse 11: "The victor shall never be harmed by the second death." What is the second death? Our first death happens when we take our last breath on earth. The second death comes to unrepented sinners at the Final Judgment, and it is eternal. But "the victor" is the Christian who suffers the first death — through persecution, martyrdom — and yet will never suffer the second death.

To Pergamum

The third letter is addressed to Pergamum. As Smyrna was a large Jewish community, Pergamum was a large pagan community just north of Smyrna. Temples to innumerable pagan gods dotted the city. The imperial cult, the worship of Caesar, dominated the cultural scene.

Verses 12-16: After commending the Pergamum Christians for keeping the faith, even in a city "where Satan has his throne," Jesus says that he is saddened that some of them "hold to the teaching of the Nicolaitans." He therefore tells them to repent; otherwise, they will be punished.

Verse 17: "To the victor I will give the hidden manna." "Hidden manna" is the food of life. It symbolizes our union with Jesus in eternal life. "I will also give him a white stone upon which is inscribed a new name." The pagans wore a stone (an amulet) around their necks which had a magic name written on it. They felt that if they knew the magic name, if they said the magic word, they would be protected from harm. Here Jesus is saying that he will give victorious Christians a white stone with his name upon it — to signify that they belong to him and are under his protection.

To Thyatira

This fourth letter is addressed to Thyatira which was southeast of Pergamum.

Verses 18-23: Jesus begins by commending the devout Christians in this city for their ever-greater efforts in recent times to remain loving and faithful. But then he refers to a Jezebel — a self-styled prophetess in their midst. (As Jezebel of old [see 1 Kings 21:1-14 and 2 Kings 9:22,30-34] led Israel into idolatry, so this new Jezebel was trying to lead the new Christians back into idolatry.) But she and her children will receive due punishment unless they repent.

Verses 24,25: On "you others . . . I place no further burden." He tells them to "hold fast to what you have until I come.'' Keep the faith and I will see you at the Second Coming.

Verses 26-29: "To the one who wins the victory, who keeps to my ways till the end, I will give authority over the nations." Jesus here promises the early Christians — and all who try to spread his message — that his power will be theirs. We have nothing to fear. With his power we can overcome all evil. And all this is symbolized by the "morning star."

Review and Discussion

1. In verse 1, Jesus "walks." What does it mean in Scripture when God "walks" among his creatures?
2. The two stages of full conversion are: _____ and _____ .
3. The Nicolaitans were guilty of _____
   _____.
4. What does the tree of life in verse 7 and Genesis 2:9 symbolize?
5. The city of Smyrna persecuted the Christians because
   _____.
6. In verse 9, why does the Lord tell the people they are rich even though they are living in tribulation?
7. What is the meaning of the following symbols?
   1) "ten days" (verse 10)
   2) "hidden manna" (verse 17)
   3) "white stone" with a new name inscribed on it (verse 17)
   4) "morning star" (verse 28)
8. In verse 11, what do the first and second deaths refer to?
   1) First death: _____ .
   2) Second death: _____ .
9. What is the consoling message of verse 26?

10. Other than money, list three other areas of modern life where people involve themselves in idolatry.

1) _____ .

2) _____ .

3) _____ .

11. What is the one major area of your life that still calls for repentance?

Moment of Prayerful Reflection

1. Read Revelation 2:18-19.
2. Meditate on the areas of your life where you are being faithful to the Lord in your deeds of love and service.

Let Us Pray

Lord Jesus, each day as we open our hearts and souls to your love and cleansing light, free us from attitudes and desires that destroy our ability to serve your name. Keep our minds focused on your way and your plan in our lives. Teach us to relish your spirit and loving concern. We give you our praise and thanksgiving today and always. Come, Lord Jesus. Amen.

Chapter 5
The Last Three Letters
(Revelation 3)

The last three letters to the churches are addressed to Sardis, Philadelphia, and Laodicea.

To Sardis

Sardis was situated southeast of Thyatira. It had a reputation for luxurious and licentious living.

Verses 1-3: Jesus censures its inhabitants for their hectic actions, warning them that they must return to their basic ideals. If they do not mend their ways, he will come like a thief in the night, as in Matthew 24:43 and Luke 12:39.

Verses 4-6: There are "a few persons" who have been faithful, and they "shall walk with me in white" — that is, their names will never be erased from "the book of the living." In the ancient world only the names of those considered to be a profit to the government were recorded in the census book called the Book of the Living. Here the Lord is saying that those who remain worthy will be in *his* Book of the Living.

To Philadelphia

Philadelphia is, of course, not in Pennsylvania but in Asia. Located southeast of Sardis, it — like Smyrna — had a very strong Jewish community.

Verses 7,8: Jesus says that he is "the holy One . . . who wields David's key." As the Messiah — out of the house of David — his key has opened the door to those in Philadelphia who "have held fast" to his word and "have not denied" his name. Because of their good deeds Jesus has left them "an open door": They are given the opportunity to proclaim the Good News because of their response to him.

Verses 9-11: Here Jesus addresses "those self-styled Jews" referred to earlier. These are the ones who — to avoid Roman persecution — excluded Jewish Christians from their midst. Then he tells the Christian community that he will keep them "safe in the time of trial," but warns them to "hold fast" to what they have lest someone rob them of their crown.

Verses 12,13: "I will make the victor a pillar in the temple of my God" is an image out of the Old Testament. It refers to the building of the heavenly new Jerusalem. Symbolically, then, these good Philadelphians are pillars of the Church of Jesus Christ.

To Laodicea

This last letter is to the city of Laodicea, which was situated southeast of Philadelphia. Large, rich, and commercially successful, it was located right at the crossroads of the circle of churches. Its inhabitants were extremely proud because they had everything they needed and more.

Verses 14-16: Because of their inordinate pride in their prestige and possessions, Jesus says: "I know you are neither hot nor cold. . . . Because you are lukewarm . . . I will spew you out of my mouth!" In modern vernacular, he is saying: "You're all wealthy; you're 'fat cats.' You think you have it made."

Verses 17,18: "You keep saying, 'I am so rich and secure that I want for nothing.' Little do you realize how wretched you are, how pitiable and poor, how blind and naked!" Jesus advises them to "buy . . . gold" (God's grace) from him if they wish to "be truly rich." They have nothing until they have the riches that Jesus brings.

Reading about Laodicea reminds us of modern America. So many people are so self-satisfied. They have it all. They're secure. They're proud as peacocks. They don't need anything or anyone. But Jesus says that you can't take it with you. This is the blind and naked curse that comes to those who think that material things will bring total security.

Verse 19: "Whoever is dear to me I reprove and chastise. . . . Repent!" Reproval is a sign of love.

Verses 20,21: This is one of the most beautiful passages of Holy Scripture: "Here I stand, knocking at the door. If anyone hears me calling and opens the door, I will enter his house and have supper with him, and he with me. I will give the victor the right to sit with me on my throne." The throne is the symbol of power. Jesus "has won the victory." He now invites us to join him. He knocks because he wants to come in. He has taken his seat beside his Father on his throne. He wants to share it with us.

Verse 22: "Let him who has ears heed the Spirit's word to the churches." These words conclude each of the seven letters, and they are a fitting conclusion to these first three chapters of the Book of Revelation. They remind us that JESUS HAS WON! And if we want to win, we must follow Jesus.

Background Review

Before we begin the second part of our study of the Book of Revelation, here is a brief review of the basic background information previously covered. This will help us to keep in mind the overall view lest we become confused when we look at the symbolic language in the rest of the Book. (The reader may want to refer back to this material often so as to keep the right perspective.)

Recall the *political and social environment* of Revelation's first-century Christians. They were suffering a double persecution.

First, beginning with Nero, there was a tremendous push for what was called the imperial cult, the worship of the emperor as god. This cult was absolutely repugnant to the Christians; they could not and would not participate. As a result the Christians were persecuted by the Roman authorities.

Second, the non-Christian Jews resented and persecuted the Christian Jews. Rome had exempted the Jewish people from participating in the imperial cult, but now the non-Christian Jews had to prove to Rome that they were strictly Jewish and did not belong to this distinct and separate religion of no specific nationality whose members called themselves "Christians." Up to that time the Christian Jews had been intermingling religious practices by going to the synagogue to participate in some of their Old Testament tradition and, then, leaving to participate in the practices and traditions of the followers of Jesus. These people were now being excluded from the Jewish centers in Asia Minor by the non-Christian Jews because the latter wanted to keep their privileges. Thus the Christian Jews suffered persecution from the non-Christian Jews.

Remember, too, the *theological theme* of the Book of Revelation: The power and justice of the risen Christ is greater than that of any human power — whether that power is exerted by pagan Rome or by non-Christian Jews as explained above. Jesus Christ is Victor. The first-century Christians sorely needed this assurance. Some Christians were beginning to think that it was safer to compromise with the opposition. They were living in a complex world, and they were tempted to yield to the power of Rome in order to avoid persecution. They wanted to follow Jesus, but they felt they could compromise whenever it was necessary. However, the Book of Revelation says, "No, you must not compromise; the power of Jesus Christ will see you through."

Lastly, recall the *ethical viewpoint* of Revelation: It summons us to commit ourselves to do away with evil in our personal lives, in the Christian community, and in the overall society. Revelation exhorts us not to compromise with evil. Time and again it reminds us that Jesus has won and salvation is ours. But it also censures those who are failing to resist the temptation to compromise. The key message here is that the entire world — whether it be Christian or not — is called to repentance; and, at the same time, it calls Christians to faithful resistance.

All these thoughts explode on our ears in a style of writing called *apocalyptic*. They resemble, as we said previously, a fireworks display on the Fourth of July. To the modern mind, the cryptic symbols seem illogical. There is no such object as a "slain lamb standing," for instance. Slain lambs don't stand. Yet, Revelation portrays a slain lamb *standing*. We might say, "There is no such thing as a slain lamb that can stand.'' And an apocalyptic writer would answer, ''So what? Whoever said there was? That is not the point.'' Revelation explodes with images; it is a dream, a series of visions.

Review and Discussion

1. Whose names will be written in ''the book of the living'' (verse 5)?

2. Why are the ''self-styled Jews,'' in verse 9, condemned?

3. How do we become ''pillars of the temple'' (verse 12)?

4. Was it material wealth alone that caused Laodicea to be condemned (verse 17)?

5. Paraphrase in your own words the beautiful passage in verses 20-21 where Jesus says he is knocking at the door of your heart.

6. What is the meaning of each of these symbols?
   1) ''David's key'' (verse 7)
   2) ''Open door'' (verse 8)

7. The first three chapters of Revelation teach us that if we want to win we must follow _____.

8. Summarize in your own words:
   1) The social and political background of the Book of Revelation
   2) The theological theme
   3) The ethical theme

9. Why do people put their trust in the security of this world instead of depending on God's providence?

10. What do the Lord's words, ''Here I stand, knocking at the door . . . . I will enter his house and have supper with him, and he with me,'' mean to you in your personal experience of the Lord?

Moment of Prayerful Reflection

1. Read Revelation 3:19-21.
2. Meditate on how much more powerful you feel when you open your mind and heart to the Lord and his inspiration.

Let Us Pray

Lord Jesus, inspire us daily to leave the doors to our hearts open to your inspiration and guidance. When we fill ourselves with self-pity and pride, knock at our hearts and teach us your way of dependence upon your Father and trust in the power of your Spirit. Move us out of self-centeredness into actions of love, forgiveness, and caring. We praise your name, Lord Jesus, and give you our love and devotion. Come, Lord Jesus. Amen.

". . . on the throne was seated One whose appearance had a gemlike sparkle. . . ."

(Revelation 4:2,3)

PART TWO

THE CHURCH COMMITTED

(Revelation 4-20)

OF HEAVEN, OF SCROLLS, OF SEALS, OF TRUMPETS, OF PLAGUES, AND OF JUDGMENT

Chapter 6
God's Worship in Heaven
(Revelation 4)

This part of the Book of Revelation will plunge us into some of the most extravagant symbols imaginable. We will examine the images to see what they mean, and, then, we will give an apocalyptic interpretation.

We discussed the difference between prophecy and apocalypse in Chapter 3, and it is good to keep this in mind throughout our study. Prophecy says, ''Repent, keep trying, you'll make it.'' Apocalypse says that Jesus has conquered, but its author vividly reminds us of what will happen to the unrepentant. Thus, Revelation shows us the power of God; he can do extraordinary things. And what is described at times seems rather gloomy, but we must remember how the story ends — with a new heaven and a new earth. Jesus will come again in power and in glory.

Chapter 4 contains no gloom whatsoever. By giving us a vision of heavenly worship, it anticipates, in a way, what will be further defined in the final two chapters.

Verse 1: "Above me there was an open door to heaven, and I heard the trumpetlike voice which had spoken to me before. It said, 'Come up here and I will show you what must take place in time to come.'" "Come up here" is an image in apocalyptic literature. It says this to us: "Come up from your world to my world. Leave the human for the divine. Separate yourselves from everything that is earthly. Come up here and I will show you the vision. You'll never see the vision down there. You're too much involved with the stuff of the human world. Come up here." This is an image that's used time and again in apocalyptic literature.

Verses 2-4: In his ecstasy, John sees "One whose appearance had a gemlike sparkle as of jasper and carnelian." Precious stones are used very often in apocalyptic literature to indicate transcendent and unbelievable beauty and power. God in heaven transcends everything here on earth.

Verses 4,5: "Surrounding this throne were twenty-four other thrones upon which were seated twenty-four elders; they were clothed in white garments and had crowns of gold on their heads." Twenty-four is a symbolic number. It represents the twelve Old Testament tribes plus the twelve apostles or the new Church. Their "white garments" are symbols of priestly garb; they have the power of prayer and the faculty to make holy and sanctify! Their "crowns of gold" signify that they are co-rulers with the Lamb! All the just in heaven rule with the Lord!

Verse 6: "The floor around the throne was like a sea of glass that was crystal-clear." Why the glass floor? Glass was very expensive in the East. It gave more than just a touch of class to the entire throne room. Glass is also reflective and transparent. In apocalyptic writing it denotes clear vision. God's perception of his world is unimpeded. He sees clearly both the good and the bad that happen here on earth.

Verse 6b-8a: "Around the throne of [God] . . . stood four living creatures covered with eyes front and back. The first creature resembled a lion, the second an ox; the third had the face of a man, while the fourth looked like an eagle in flight. Each . . . had six wings and eyes all over, inside and out."

The four creatures are similar to those described by Ezekiel (1:10). Symbolically, they represent the four corners of the world surrounding the Creator. Their "eyes front and back" indicate that they make sure that God sees all. Each of the creatures also represents a quality of Christ: the lion, nobility; the ox, strength; man, wisdom; and the eagle, swiftness. God is noble. He is strong. He is wise. He is swift (prompt) in caring for his creation.

Later, the Church will assign these same symbols to the evangelists: Matthew, the man; Mark, the lion; Luke, the ox; and John, the eagle. We see them represented in this way in many art forms.

Verses 8b,9: "Day and night, without pause, they sing:
   Holy, holy, holy, is the Lord God Almighty,
   He who was, and who is, and who is to come!"
This is what the neo-apocalyptics of today, the prophets of doom, keep emphasizing; and this is why they have an audience. For the God whom the elders praise is the Lord of history. Using this as their basis, the modern-day prophets of doom then spin their web of conjecture of how God is involved in the history of the twentieth century.

Verses 10,11: "The twenty-four elders fall down before" God and worship him, singing another song of praise to him who has "created all things." These "twenty-four" represent the entire People of God. Their falling down and throwing down their crowns are symbolic actions of homage. To bow down or to kneel down indicates payment of homage. To throw down one's crown is to say, "I have no power except the power you give to me.'' We think of Napoleon who — in the nineteenth century — did just the opposite. He took the crown from the pope and put it on his own head! Napoleon was saying to the pope, ''You don't give me power. I bestow power on myself.''

Review and Discussion

1. Although much gloom is depicted in Revelation, how does the story end?
2. In verse 1, ''Come up here'' is an image calling us to come up from _____ to _____ .
3. What is the meaning of each of these symbols?
   1) ''precious stones'' (verse 3)
   2) ''twenty-four'' (verse 4)
   3) ''crowns of gold'' (verse 4)
   4) ''sea of glass'' (verse 6)
4. What does each of the four creatures resemble in verses 6 and 7?
   1) First: _____ .
   2) Second: _____ .
   3) Third: _____ .
   4) Fourth: _____ .
5. In verse 8, why do the four creatures have eyes all over?
6. The four creatures symbolize characteristics of the Lord. What does each symbolize?
   1) The lion: _____ .
   2) The ox: _____ .
   3) The man: _____ .
   4) The eagle: _____ .
7. Which creature represents which evangelist?
   1) Matthew: _____ .
   2) Mark: _____ .
   3) Luke: _____ .
   4) John: _____ .

8. What image in verse 10 is used to symbolize homage to the Lord?
9. What "earthly" temptations are keeping you from "coming up to the Lord"?
10. What experiences of the Lord have you had that would lead you to praise him?

Moment of Prayerful Meditation

1. Read Revelation 4:11.
2. Meditate on why the Lord God deserves to receive your personal honor and praise.

Let Us Pray

Lord Jesus, you are all holy and good and worthy of our praise, honor, and thanksgiving. You love and forgive and inspire. Your glory and power reach unto the ends of the universe. Your way is our Way! Your gift of salvation is our eternal hope. May we always be faithful messengers of your word. We praise you, Creator and Sustainer of all life, forever and ever. Come, Lord Jesus. Amen.

Chapter 7
The Scroll and the Lamb
(Revelation 5)

Revelation 5 tells the story of the sealed scroll which could be opened only by the Lamb. That Jesus is the Lamb is revealed in symbolic language.

Verses 1-4: "In the right hand of the One who sat on the throne I saw a scroll. It had writing on both sides and was sealed with seven seals." Remember the number seven? It denotes completeness. So here it could mean that the scroll was totally sealed. (Note that for many centuries now we have had seven sacraments. This signifies that the totality of Jesus is present with us throughout our lives. From the moment we are baptized — through every stage of life, even to the moment when we prepare for the afterlife with the Sacrament of the Sick — Jesus is totally present to us.)

This scroll, which "no one in heaven or on earth or under the earth" could open, was similar to the documents used in ancient times. When scribes wrote a document in those days they would seal it in a container. Thus properly sealed, the document was now official. That it was "written on both sides" — which was practically impossible, given the material at hand — poses a problem. We do know, however, that what was contained in the sealed scroll was God's plan for the history of the world. The Second Coming is on the scroll, and it is perfectly sealed so that nobody knows the secret except the One who has the power to open it. John then says, "I wept bitterly because no one could be found worthy to open or examine the scroll."

Verses 5,6: "One of the elders said to me: 'Do not weep. The Lion of the tribe of Judah, the Root of David, has won the right by his victory to open the scroll with the seven seals.' " What is he telling us? The "Lion" and the "Root" are messianic titles applied to Christ. So, Jesus is the revelation of what God is going to do in history, age after age. Jesus is the living revelation of the scroll — God's plan of action throughout history. We, then, know to some degree God's plan for the world because we see Jesus at work in every age.

If someone tells us that the scroll referred to here in Revelation reveals that God on the Last Day will destroy all people whether they are good or bad, we cannot believe them. God's plan for the history of the world can be known only by his Son, as revealed to him by his Father.

To summarize what has been symbolized here: The sealed scroll describes how God deals in history with creation. The One who can open the scroll is Jesus Christ. God is his Father, so Jesus knows how God acts. And we know how Jesus acts. We know how he reacts. We not only read about this in the Gospels, we also experience it in our own personal lives. *We know.* Therefore, when we are told — by doomsday writers, for example — that God will do something contrary to what Jesus did as described in the Gospels, we know that such an assertion is erroneous.

John now continues. "Then, between the throne with the four living creatures and the elders, I saw a Lamb standing, a Lamb that had been slain." Jesus — the Lamb (see John 1:29) — stands between God and humankind. By his death and Resurrection he has acted as mediator. As a slain Lamb he bears the marks of his Passion; yet, he stands before the world as the risen Lord, the Lamb of God who took away the sins of the world.

Jesus — as Lamb — is then further described as having "seven horns and seven eyes." A horn is like a crown. The ancient kings used to take the horn of a bull and hold it up before their assembly as a sign of their power. Jesus has *seven* horns: He has full power. He has *seven* eyes: He has infinite wisdom and knowledge.

Verses 7-11: "The Lamb came and received the scroll from the right hand of the One who sat on the throne." The ancient kings sat, and their chief functionaries always sat at their right hand. The Father sits on the throne, and his Son Jesus now sits at his right hand. His acceptance of the scroll signifies that he has received full authority and is now the Lord of the universe. He has been given that power by his Father. Then the whole assembly — the four living creatures and the twenty-four elders — fall down in worship before the Lamb, as they offer the prayers of God's holy people. And they sing a hymn extolling the slain Lamb whose blood had redeemed the entire world.

Verses 12-14: "And they all cried out:
  'Worthy is the Lamb that was slain
    to receive power and riches, wisdom and strength,
    honor and glory and praise!' "
Countless angels and every living creature joined the rest of the assembly in this joyous acclamation and the following one, which heaped praise, honor, and glory on the Father and the Son. We, too, owe them the same homage.

So, never fear about the opening of the seals. Jesus is Lord of the universe. We know him from the Gospels. True, when he comes he will pass judgment. But if we accept his warnings here in Revelation, we will resist the temptation to compromise with pagan values and will appear before him as repentant Christians.

Review and Discussion

1. Recall the theological theme of Revelation.
2. The number "seven" symbolizes _____ .
3. How do we know the scroll was an official document?
4. What was contained in the scroll?
5. In verse 4, why did John weep?
6. Who is the revelation of God to mankind?
7. How does seeing Jesus in action in the Gospels help us interpret the imagery in the Book of Revelation?
8. In verse 6, the "slain lamb standing" is _____ . He is standing between the throne and the elders and creatures because _____ .
9. What does the "slain lamb standing" symbolize?
10. In verse 6, what do "seven horns" and "seven eyes" indicate?
11. What image is used in verse 7 to teach us that Jesus is the Lord of the universe?
12. Why does John proclaim Jesus as Lord before he describes what happens when the seals are opened?
13. What do you feel God's plan is for you right now in your life?
14. What do you do to show the Lord that he is first in your life and your decisions?

Moment of Prayerful Reflection

1. Read Revelation 5:9-10.
2. Meditate on what you feel God's plan is for you at this moment in the history of your personal life.

Let Us Pray

Lord Jesus, you alone know the meaning and purpose of our lives. Give us your insight. Lead us to follow your way of self-sacrifice and love so that we may live in your peace and joy. You have called us to be your people, to serve you and each other. Give us courage and creativity to help build your Kingdom. We give you our praise and adoration all the days of our lives. Come, Lord Jesus. Amen.

Chapter 8
The First Six Seals
(Revelation 6)

This is perhaps the best remembered chapter of Revelation because the first four seals concern the Four Horsemen. Football fans are reminded of the "Four Horsemen" of Notre Dame. Movie enthusiasts will recall *Apocalypse Now.* We should keep in mind throughout this entire section that the vivid description of the agony of the unjust is always followed by the ecstasy of the just. The first six seals in this chapter depict death and destruction, but before the seventh seal is opened the joy and gladness of the elect is portrayed. And the whole book concludes with a rapturous rehearsal of the new heavens and the new earth. Perhaps John, like many a reporter, became so carried away by the evil he saw that he wrote more of the "bad" than the "good" news.

Verses 1,2: "The Lamb broke open the first of the seven seals . . . I saw a white horse; its rider had a bow, and . . . a crown." The bow and the crown represent military power. "He rode forth victorious." The first horseman symbolizes *conquering power*.

Verses 3,4: "The Lamb broke open the second seal." This time a red horse appeared. Its rider had "a huge sword" — "to rob the earth of peace." The second horseman symbolizes *war*.

Verses 5,6: The third seal reveals a black horse, whose rider "held a pair of scales in his hand." Then John says, "I heard what seemed to be a voice coming from in among the four living creatures. It said: 'A day's pay for a ration of wheat and the same for three of barley! But spare the olive oil and the wine!' " And what — for goodness sake — does all that mean? The third horseman symbolizes *famine*. During the time of famine it costs a fortune to buy even basic food — a whole day's wage just for a little barley and a little wheat. In today's world, let's suppose that a man earns ten dollars an hour. To buy one box of Wheaties would cost him eighty dollars! And what is the meaning of "Spare the olive oil and the wine"? It means, "Don't waste your time destroying these things." If the people can't buy wheat, they certainly won't be able to afford champagne. The famine described here is devastating.

Verses 7,8: Out of the fourth seal comes a sickly green horse. "Its rider was named Death." The fourth horseman symbolizes *death*. "These four [riders] were given authority over one quarter of the earth." In apocalyptic writing, when a number is cut into a fraction, that denotes incompleteness. So here, God is in control. He determines how much is done by the evil forces of the world. He limits them. He checks them. He binds them. (Later on we shall see that he binds Satan.)

Verses 9-11: When the fifth seal was broken John "saw under the altar the spirits of those who had been martyred because of the witness they bore to the word of God." These were crying out: "How long will it be, O Master, holy and true, before you judge our cause?" Each was then given a long white robe — as a symbol of victory — and "were told to be patient a little while longer." This was good news for the early Christians, and it is good news for us today. If we continue to patiently resist evil — signified here by war, famine, and death — we will conquer even as Jesus conquered.

These martyrs had stayed faithful. They resisted compromise. They refused to despair. They believed that Jesus was Victor.

This is a stimulating, comforting message for all of us today: "Don't despair. Don't fall apart. Don't say, 'Why bother anymore?' " Jesus says, "Be patient. You know I love you." What is the general theological meaning here? The Lord knows that evil exists in the world. He allows it to exist. But he promises that evil will not win out. He has won the victory; and, if we remain with him, we will win too!

Verses 12-17: These verses that follow on the breaking of the sixth seal are a symbolic rather than a literal description of what will happen on the day of the Lord. They are extremely vivid: the earth quakes, the sun turns black, the moon glows red as blood, the sky disappears, and every mountain and island is uprooted. They symbolize social evils.

After the cosmic upheavals just described, all the people on earth hide themselves "from the wrath of the Lamb." Why? Because they realize their sinfulness. Adam and Eve also hid from God after the first sin.

Review and Discussion

1. What do each of the Four Horsemen symbolize?
   1) First: _____ .
   2) Second: _____ .
   3) Third: _____ .
   4) Fourth: _____ .
2. In the description of the white horse (verse 2), what do the "bow" and the "crown" symbolize?
3. What is the meaning of verses 5 and 6 in this chapter?
4. What is the meaning of "authority over one-fourth of the earth" in verse 8?
5. In verse 11, what do the "white robes" symbolize?
6. What virtue do we learn from verse 11?
7. Why do the people described in verse 15 run and hide?
8. How does believing in Jesus help you personally not to despair?
9. What elements in your life do you try to hide from the Lord?

Moment of Prayerful Reflection

1. Read Revelation 6:3-4.
2. Meditate on what in your attitude and behavior robs peace from the lives of those around you.

Let Us Pray

Lord Jesus, only in you do we find lasting peace and the way to live in peace with each other. Forgive us of the things we say and do that destroy peace between us. Show us the way to accept those around us and to foster peace, forgiveness, and understanding. We acknowledge that only in your power are we able to live lives of peace. Help us to live your way. We give you praise for loving and forgiving us. Come, Lord Jesus. Amen.

Chapter 9
Sealing of the Thousands
(Revelation 7)

This chapter forms a kind of interlude between the opening of the first six seals and the opening of the seventh and final seal. It is a welcome respite between the woes just described and those which will immediately follow. Two joyful scenes are portrayed here: the servants of God and the victorious martyrs receive their reward.

Verse 1: "After this I saw four angels standing at the four corners of the earth; they held in check the earth's four winds so that no wind blew on land or sea or through any tree." The ancients presumed the world was a disk or rectangle surrounded by water. The water and land were inside a bowl. At the top of the bowl, stars hung like baubles from a Christmas tree. God was up on top of the bowl, and Satan was in the depths of the earth — the underworld. From their corner positions the four angels hold in check the winds from the north, south, east, and west.

Verses 2,3: "I saw another angel come up from the east holding the seal of the living God." East, in symbolic language, is the direction from which salvation comes. From the east comes the rising sun, and from the east comes the light of salvation. The seal in the angel's hand is God's plan for the world. He cries out to the other angels to continue holding back the winds until he imprints his seal "on the foreheads of the servants of our God." Imprinting with a seal is an ancient custom. Warm wax receives the impress of a ring, for example, and the resulting imprint indicates ownership and promises protection. In a similar way, these "servants of God" receive their seal of approval.

Verses 4-8: "I heard the number of those who were so marked — one hundred and forty-four thousand." (The twelve tribes of Israel squared equals one hundred and forty-four thousand.) This is not a literal but a symbolic number. It means that a limitless number will be sealed with salvation. Why? Because there will be a limitless number of people — of every race and nation — who will listen to the Lord.

Verses 9-12: "I saw before me a huge crowd which no one could count from every nation and race, people and tongue. They stood before the throne and the Lamb, dressed in long white robes and holding palm branches in their hands. They cried out in a loud voice, 'Salvation is from our God, who is seated on the throne, and from the Lamb!' " And the whole assembly "fell down before the throne to worship God," while singing praise to his name.

Verses 13,14: One of the elders then explains that these white-robed people are "the ones who have survived the great period of trial; they have washed their robes and made them white in the blood of the Lamb." These are the martyrs who suffered persecution out of love for the Lamb.

Verses 15-17: These martyrs minister to God in his temple forever.

"Never again shall they know hunger or thirst,
  nor shall the sun or its heat beat down on them."

The Lamb will shepherd them, leading them "to springs of life-giving water [God's grace], and God will wipe every tear from their eyes." This is the promise already fulfilled by the early Christian martyrs. And it is extended to us today. All we need do is to follow Jesus, the Good Shepherd. His Church stands ready to fortify us with the living water of the sacraments as we journey on our way to meet the early Christian martyrs.

Review and Discussion

1. What is the overall message of this chapter?
2. What does the word *east* symbolize?
3. The angel from the east holds the _____ in his hands.
4. Explain the meaning of sealing the foreheads of the servants of God.
5. Is the number one hundred and forty-four thousand literal or symbolic? Explain.
6. Who are the elect described in verses 9 to 14?
7. What are the promises made to the martyrs in verses 16 and 17?
8. In our day, what are life-giving waters?
9. Have you ever experienced the protecting power of God? If so, describe how you felt.

Moment of Prayerful Reflection

1. Read Revelation 7:13,14.
2. Meditate on how the Lord has protected you and has led you through past trials and difficulties.

Let Us Pray

Lord Jesus, you who know what it is to suffer tribulation and persecution, aid us with your loving protection. Help us to commend our lives to your Father's Spirit as you did. May we grow in our appreciation of depending totally on the will and love of our Father. Inspire us to reach out to others who are suffering and share our lives and gifts. We give you praise and honor and glory for all time. Come, Lord Jesus. Amen.

Chapter 10
The Seventh Seal
and the First Six Trumpets
(Revelation 8 and 9)

After the welcome respite of the last chapter, which described the joyous rewards of those who are sealed as the servants of God, John returns here to the doleful account of the woes that will beset the world before the Second Coming. (Some say that John may have been overly pessimistic in his account.) He begins with the opening of the seventh seal.

Revelation 8

Verse 1: "When the Lamb broke open the seventh seal, there was silence in heaven for about half an hour." What does that mean? Its purpose is to emphasize the solemnity of the act that God is about to perform. We are on pins and needles as we wait to see what will happen. Suspense is an integral part of apocalyptic literature.

Verses 2-5: After the proper time has elapsed, seven angels are given seven trumpets. (Trumpets are symbols of divine action.) Then another angel holding a censer "took his place at the altar of incense" and added large amounts of incense. "The smoke of the incense went up before God, and with it the prayers of God's people." (Yes, there *are* angels, and they *do* intercede for us with God.) "Then the angel took the censer, filled it with live coals . . . and hurled it down to the earth." And, amid thunder and lightning, "the earth trembled." This last action symbolizes judgment. But the early Christians took heart on hearing this passage: They knew that their prayers were being heard and that the punishment just described was to fall not on them but on their persecutors.

We, too, can learn much from this vision — especially in the area of punishment. Actually, God does not have to punish us; we punish ourselves. I remember when I was a small child how my mother used to punish me when I was bad. There was a belt that hung in the closet in the hallway. I would have to get a chair to reach it because it hung on a nail far above my head. She would say, "Go get the belt. Go get it and bring it to me." On my way to the closet, I would stop in the bathroom, go make my bed, feed the dog, read a couple of comic books . . . and in about ten minutes she'd say, "I'm waiting!" I would finally get there, and she'd take the belt and say, "OK, go put it back." Whew! She never touched me with the belt. It was years before I figured out what she was doing. I'd already gone through the punishment — just by going to get the belt. She didn't have to touch me! God lets us punish ourselves in much the same way.

Verses 6-12: The four catastrophes that happen here when each angel blows his trumpet are reminiscent of the plagues of Egypt. Each one affects nature and creation in some way: the *land* and plant life (verse 7); the *sea,* the creatures of the sea, and the ships at sea (verses 8,9); the *rivers and springs* (verses 10,11); the *sun, moon, and stars* (verse 12). Now, in each case, one-third of the designated area is affected. Why one-third? When a definite fraction is used in this type of literature it means "not totally." It implies a warning. God wants us to repent. In a way, it's like my mother saying: "Go get the belt and bring it to me." God wants us to think things over.

Verse 13: "I heard an eagle flying in midheaven cry out in a loud voice, 'Woe, woe, and again woe to the inhabitants of earth from the trumpet blasts the other three angels are about to blow!'" The "eagle" symbolizes swiftness. It flies "in midheaven" so that when it screams the message can be heard all over the universe.

The description of the disasters that follow upon the first four trumpet blasts forces us to ask ourselves: "What is the source of all this power?" I was reminded of this when I visited Vancouver, Washington, after Mount Saint Helens erupted. A nun there had a bottle of volcanic ashes resting on her desk. Wrapped around the bottle was a piece of paper with these written words: "The Lord is my Savior." Imagine her sitting there when all of a sudden a mountain blows up! "My God!" she explains. He replies, "Precisely. Did a good job, huh? Precisely! I got all of you thinking about me, didn't I? Worked very well, didn't it?" So, here in this chapter and in the following one these earthshaking events are meant to wake people up and make them cry out, "Who can control this?" And God answers: "Turn to me. I can control it. I'm just trying to show you."

Revelation 9

This ninth chapter continues with the fifth and sixth symbolic disasters. These will affect humankind more directly.

Verses 1-6: "Then the fifth angel blew his trumpet, and I saw a star [an angel] fall from the sky to the earth. The star was given the key to the shaft of the abyss." The abyss refers to *sheol*, which, in Jewish theology, is the abode of the dead. It was believed to be underneath the earth with a shaft leading down to it. The shaft was sealed over. So, God is saying, "Here's the key. Unlock the shaft. Go down into the abyss and let the demons out. They will shake up the world, and then maybe it will shape up." Out came the demons, then, in the form of scorpionlike locusts. The smoke that accompanied them darkened the sun and the air. Locusts were — and still are — a terrible curse in the Middle East because they destroyed the crops. But these locusts were told "to do no harm to the grass in the land or to any plant or tree but only to those men who had not the seal of God on their foreheads." The curse, then, is limited: Do not kill them; "only . . . torture them for five months." This, of course, sounds strange to us; locusts have never been known to discriminate in the past nor do they do so in the present. They destroy everything in their path. But, remember, God is controlling this whole event. He has *all* authority and *all* power. And the "five months"? This agonizing torture of sinners will last for that length of time — the approximate life-span of locusts.

Verses 7-11: If we think that the creatures we may have seen in horror films are outlandish, this passage will help us change our minds. The locusts wore crowns of gold. "Their faces were like men's faces but they had hair like women's hair. The teeth were the teeth of lions, their chests like iron breastplates. Their wings made a sound like the roar of many chariots and horses charging into battle. They had tails with stingers like scorpions." This imagery comes right out of a nightmare. It is as if God is saying "I'm doing everything I can to make you see the importance of repentance."

There is an important lesson here for all of us. If we have been sealed, the agony just described will not be ours. And how do we know whether we are sealed? God is telling us that if we follow Jesus by feeding the hungry, clothing the naked, and visiting the sick and the imprisoned, we have the mark of true Christians. By sharing with others the fullness of what we have we are sealed. Yes, evil will continue to surround us; but if we are sealed, we will not be destroyed.

Verses 12-15: After the sixth angel blew his trumpet, John heard a voice saying: "Release the four angels who are tied up on the banks of the great river Euphrates." They are released, and they prepare "to kill a third of mankind." Evil can't win all the time, so the Lord sets a day for its destruction. He is in control. Now, at the time when the Book of Revelation was written, the greatest threat to Rome was the Parthian Empire, which was located right on the eastern shore of the Euphrates River. The allusion here is to the tremendous power of the Parthian army. It is the "white horse" of the Four Horsemen. And the symbolic invasion is permitted by God to punish Rome for the persecution of Christians.

Verses 16-19: The troops from the Euphrates — "whose count I heard, were two hundred million in number" — were cavalry troops. People who start figuring here, "Let's see, how many soldiers does Russia have now?" will go insane. That's not what John is talking about. "Two hundred million" simply means that the invasion will be more than human; it will be superhuman. Apocalyptic literature likes to exaggerate. This passage then concludes with a vivid description of the cavalry — men's horses breathing "smoke and sulphur and fire" — to indicate their ferocity.

Verses 20,21: "That part of mankind which escaped the plagues did not repent of the idols they had made. They did not give up the worship of demons, or of gods made from gold and silver, from bronze and stone and wood, which cannot see or hear or walk. Neither did they repent of their murders or their sorcery, their fornication or their thefts." The literal meaning of "the idols they had made" is "the works of their hands." So, the reference here is not just to man-made idols worshiped as gods but also to any sinful action — even those not mentioned in the final verse. We can, therefore, imagine God speaking to us today in the following manner:

"Everything that you are and have comes to you from me. All that I have is yours. I love you, and all that I ask in return is your love. You prove your love for me by loving each other and forgiving one another. But if you are jealous and vengeful, it's apparent you don't love me. So, I remind you now — even as I reminded the early Christians — that war, famine, and pestilence will continue in your world until you begin to think of me and begin to follow my Son. So many of you never think of me at all. When you get a raise you say: 'How nice of the boss!' But if you happen to lose your job, you say: 'Why me, God?' If anything good comes about, *you* claim it was *your* doing. If any evil comes about, it's *my* doing. You don't turn to me unless you begin to fall apart. And some of you don't even turn to me then! What am I to do?"

Review and Discussion

1. What does each of the following images symbolize?
   1) "half an hour" (8:1)
   2) "hurled it [the censer] down to the earth" (8:5)
   3) "one-third" (8:7-12)
   4) "eagle in midheaven" (8:13)
   5) "shaft of the abyss" (9:1)
   6) "five months" (9:10)

2. In 8:3, when the angel put more incense on the altar, what did that signify?
3. Name the four disasters that each of the first four trumpets announced.
    1) _____ .
    2) _____ .
    3) _____ .
    4) _____ .
4. What people were spared from the plague of the locusts (9:4)?
5. Why does the Lord permit all these disasters?
6. In 9:15, what were the four released angels prepared to do?
7. Is there a message for today's world in 9:20,21?
8. What should you do to overcome the apathy and sinfulness of today's world?
9. What "messengers" does the Lord use in your personal life to remind you of what he has called you to be?

Moment of Prayerful Reflection

1. Read Revelation 9:20,21.
2. Meditate on your need to repent and to put aside anything that is separating you from deep union with the Lord.

Let Us Pray

Lord Jesus, you show us the way to intimate union with you, the Father, and the Spirit. Help us to clarify our actions and thoughts so as to produce lives of love, sacrifice, and acceptance of our total dependence on the loving will of the Father. Fill us with your spirit of truth, peace, and compassion. We lift our hearts to you in praise and adoration. Come, Lord Jesus. Amen.

Chapter 11
The Little Scroll
(Revelation 10)

Once again, in this chapter and the beginning of the next, we have a welcome interruption before the seventh disaster is described. These two scenes are meant to restore the spirit of the early Christians. But before we begin, recall the central message, the total scope of Revelation: *Jesus has conquered! He is the Victor!* And despite the disasters that have fallen and will fall on the world, the faithful who continue to follow the humble path of the Carpenter from Nazareth will win out and reign with Jesus forever. So, we must not allow all the symbols and the wild Fourth of July experiences that John encounters in his visions to trap us. Abide in Jesus the Redeemer. This is the message of the Book of Revelation, whether we are talking about two thousand years ago, one thousand years ago, three hundred years ago, today, fifteen hundred years from now, or three thousand years from now.

Verse 1: John's previous visions happened in heaven — in the throne room before God and the Lamb and the elders.

However, these two scenes take place here on earth. "Then I saw another mighty angel come down from heaven wrapped in a cloud, with a rainbow about his head; his face shone like the sun and his legs like pillars of fire." The images here — a cloud, a rainbow, the sun, pillars of fire — remind us of how our Lord looked at his Transfiguration.

Verses 2,3: "In his hand he held a little scroll which had been opened." The *big* scroll with the seven seals (in 5:1) had been sealed. That this scroll was "little" indicates that only a small part of God's plan for the world is to be revealed. "He placed his right foot on the sea and his left foot on the land." Land and sea cover the entire universe. The message, then, is for the entire world. The angel "gave a loud cry like the roar of a lion [power]. When he cried out, the seven thunders raised their voices too." Thunder, as a symbol, recalls the event at Mount Sinai in the Old Testament when God gave the commandments to Moses and thunder pealed. This is an Old Testament image of God's power at work. I remember when I was a small child how my grandmother made us light candles in the window when it thundered. We did it because God was at hand, and we had to watch out!

Verses 4-7: "I was about to start writing when the seven thunders spoke, but I heard a voice from heaven say, 'Seal up what the seven thunders have spoken and do not write it down!'" This probably is a further indication that God wants only part of his plan revealed. "Then the angel . . . took an oath by the One who lives forever and ever. . . . 'There shall be no more delay.'" The forces of evil are to be destroyed. The time of deliverance is at hand. "When the time comes for the seventh angel to blow his trumpet, the mysterious plan of God, which he announced to his servants the prophets, shall be accomplished in full." God's plan for the entire world will be accomplished. Jesus' victory will be total. So, once again we return to our theme: Jesus is Victor. He will accomplish everything in full.

Verses 8-10: "Then the voice which I heard from heaven spoke to me again and said, 'Go take the open scroll from the hand of the angel. . . . ' " So, John approached the angel and asked for the scroll. And the angel said: "Here, take it and eat it! It will be sour in your stomach, but in your mouth it will taste as sweet as honey." John then took the scroll; and it *did* taste sweet in his mouth, and it *did* turn sour in his stomach.

Although the above passage sounds strange, its symbolism is quite clear. When we eat something we consume it; it becomes a part of our very selves. John consumes the message entirely, and it is now totally his to proclaim. That it was sweet to the taste indicates that its contents were pleasant to absorb. And what did it contain? The disclosure that Christ will be victorious and so will be his faithful followers. That it was sour to the stomach signifies that Christians must be ready to accept suffering and sacrifice. Christ himself claimed victory only after he suffered and died on the Cross.

If we are to follow Jesus and come to resurrection and life, we have to take up our cross to follow him. Taking up our cross is not sweet; it is sour or bitter, and it is difficult to do. However, if we do take up our cross and bear it, we will win the victory under the leadership of Christ the Victor.

Verse 11: "Then someone said to me, 'You must prophesy again for many peoples and nations, languages and kings.' " This means that the message revealed to John is intended for the whole world. All the world will suffer, but those who follow Christ will triumph because of his power and because of his ability to turn everything into good. The message is for all, not just to the Christian community.

Review and Discussion

1. Once again, what three words summarize the basic teaching of Revelation?
2. In verse 2, what does the "little scroll" symbolize?
3. What does the symbol of the angel placing his right foot on the sea and his left foot on the land (10:2) mean?
4. Thunder (in verse 3) is used in Scripture as a symbol of
   _____ .
5. Why does the message of verse 7 fill us with confidence?
6. Explain the symbolism of "eating the scroll" (verse 10).
7. Explain the meaning of "sweet as honey" (verse 9).
8. Explain the meaning of "sour to the stomach" (verse 10).
9. What words in verse 11 teach us that the Lord's message is universal?
10. What "crosses" do you have today in your life that need Jesus' loving help?

Moment of Prayerful Reflection

1. Read Revelation 10:9.
2. Meditate on how you are living your commitment to Jesus and when it is a joy and when it is a problem.

Let Us Pray

Lord Jesus, you show us by your life how to be dedicated to the plan of your Father, a plan of love and acceptance. Your crucifixion reminds us of how far we must go in our love of others. Your Resurrection gives us hope and consolation. Inspire us today to live in a loving and caring way with all people so as to feel your peace and give you glory. We praise you, Lord, and love you today and always. Come, Lord Jesus. Amen.

Chapter 12
The Two Witnesses
and the Seventh Trumpet
(Revelation 11)

Our interlude before the blast of the seventh trumpet continues in the first part of this chapter.

Verses 1,2: "Someone gave me a measuring rod, and said: 'Come and take the measurements of God's temple and altar, and count those who worship there. Exclude the outer court of the temple, however; do not measure it, for it has been handed over to the Gentiles, who will crush the holy city for forty-two months.' "

The "temple" in this passage refers to the Christian community formed initially from the old Jewish community. It symbolizes God's chosen people. In scriptural language, to "measure" something is to put it under the ownership or the protection of the master. John is, in effect, being asked to number those who belong to the Christian community so that God can protect them during the coming persecution.

But John is told not to measure the court of the Gentiles. This outer court in the temple was reserved for nonbelievers. Gentiles symbolize the unfaithful ones, the pagans of the world, "who will crush the holy city for forty-two months." Forty-two months, by the way, is twelve hundred and sixty days, or three and one-half years. This corresponds to the length of the persecution suffered by the Jews, as recorded in chapters 7 through 12 in Daniel. But it is also a fractional number of years; and, therefore, in apocalyptic language, it symbolizes a limited time. So, God is in control. Persecution will come, but the Creator and Master of the universe is in command. God is total power.

It is very important to remember this when we read about the horrendous beasts and the plagues and catastrophes depicted here. The Book of Revelation was not written to lead people to despair but to lead them to awe. In spite of all the unbelievable plagues recorded in these pages, the Lamb is victorious. This fact takes on a significant meaning for us when we examine the "plagues" of our own personal lives. We know that someone has power over the plagues that pester our lives. It is Jesus, the risen Lord. He knows what's going on. He will win. So, no matter how the "modern prophets of doom" interpret these "plagues," their predictions will not bother us because we know who is going to win. The 2,000-year-old interpretation of the Catholic Church still stands. How others interpret this splendid Book of Revelation is their business. If we follow Jesus, we can't lose. This is the message of the Book of Revelation. United with Jesus, we win.

Verses 3-5: "I will commission my two witnesses to prophesy for those twelve hundred and sixty days, dressed in sackcloth." If these "two witnesses" indicate Old Testament people, probably Moses and Elijah are meant; if they indicate New Testament people, Peter and Paul — who represent all Christian martyrs — are perhaps meant. The olive trees and the lampstands mentioned in this passage refer to the leaders of the Church and the Christian community. The "sackcloth," of course, indicates repentance. "If anyone tries to harm them, fire will come out of the mouths of these witnesses to devour their enemies." In Scripture, fire has many connotations. Here, as in Jeremiah 5:14, fire refers to the Word of God.

Verse 6: The references here to various plagues harp back to the time of Moses. The Church, if she so desired, could exercise her power to bring on like disasters. So, we can read from all this that Jesus, who is the Light of the world, will continue to guide and protect his Church, the People of God, the faithful ones who make up what is called the Mystical Body.

Verses 7,8: "When they have finished giving their testimony, the wild beast . . . from the abyss will wage war against them and conquer and kill them. Their corpses will lie in the streets of the great city, which has the symbolic name 'Sodom' or 'Egypt,' where also their Lord was crucified." Nero, the Roman emperor, is the "wild beast." The "great city" is Babylon, that is, Rome. Pagan Rome is Sodom, a symbol of moral corruption, and Egypt, a symbol of oppression. So, John is saying that Rome is the source of the persecution in the Church.

"Where also their Lord was crucified" points to Rome, where the Christians were being fed to the lions. The body of Christ was crucified in Jerusalem, but the Body of Christ — the mystical Body of Christ — was crucified in Rome. And that same resurrected Christ is in us, seated where we sit, walking where we walk, all over the world. We are the risen Lord, the Mystical Body of Christ so beautifully expounded in the encyclical by Pope Pius XII. Remember too (in Acts

9:4-5) when Paul — then known as Saul — was on his way to Damascus and what the Lord said to him? "Saul, Saul, why do you persecute me?" And what was Saul doing? He was killing Christians. Then, when Saul asked, "Who are you?" the voice answered, "I am Jesus, the one you are persecuting." This is a clear statement of the meaning of the Mystical Body.

Verse 9: The reference to "three-and-a-half days," in this verse, once again symbolizes incompleteness. For the Jews, not to bury the dead was the ultimate insult to the human person. Not burying the witnesses of Jesus symbolizes the intense hatred that the pagan world had for Christians. This hatred that the Roman Empire had for the followers of the Carpenter of Nazareth came to an unbelievable climax during the persecution by Domitian, a persecution which John and all the Christian community were experiencing. It is this persecution he refers to in the Book of Revelation.

Verse 10: "The earth's inhabitants gloat over them and in their merriment exchange gifts, because these two prophets harassed everyone on earth." The Roman authorities and the whole pagan community feel relieved because they think that never again will they have to listen to the Christian message. They are *relieved* by the destruction of the messengers of Jesus of Nazareth. How pathetic!

Yet, this same kind of reaction is seen in our own time. I remember a certain documentary which showed one of Hitler's top henchmen being interviewed. The German people had been under tremendous psychological pressure to make them believe that the Jews had caused all of Germany's problems. This henchman, when he was asked "How did you feel?" replied, *"Relieved* that the scourge was gone and at peace with myself that I had done a good thing." How horrible! During the reign of Domitian, there was the same kind of feeling on the part of pagan Rome about the followers of Jesus.

Verses 11-14: "But after the three and a half days," the witnesses returned to life; and, amid the "sheer terror" of the onlookers, they "went up to heaven in a cloud." After a short period of time, those persecuted and killed will rise with power. Next, following a violent earthquake (symbolizing social or spiritual upheaval) seven thousand people (indicating an enormous number) were killed. Then this passage ends rather strangely. Most of Revelation emphasized the unwillingness of pagans to receive Christ's message, but here they "were so terrified that they worshiped the God of heaven."

Verses 15-18: Now the seventh trumpet announces the coming of God's Kingdom: "The kingdom of the world now belongs to our Lord and to his Anointed One, and he shall reign forever and ever." Then the whole assembly of heaven "fell down to worship God" — in praise of him for rewarding the just and punishing the unjust.

Verse 19: "Then God's temple in heaven opened and in the temple could be seen the ark of his covenant." In Old Testament times, the Israelites carried the symbols of the covenant in the ark. For forty years they had carried it, from Egypt to the Promised Land. It symbolized God's presence in their midst. We feel the same way today. We walk in the door of the church and we know that — through the liturgy of the Mass — God is present in the tabernacle on our altar. When we come into our churches, we have a special feeling, don't we? We know of God's presence in the Blessed Sacrament even as the ancient Jews felt his presence in the Ark of the Covenant. This final verse symbolizes God's presence in the midst of his people, as he was in ancient Jewish history, and that he is working with them.

Review and Discussion

1. In verse 1 of this chapter, the temple is identified with the _____ at the time John is writing.

2. To measure something in scriptural language is to _____ .

3. Why is John asked to "measure the temple"?

4. Why did the Lord tell John not to measure the outer courts of the temple?

5. What do "forty-two months," "one-third," and "twelve hundred and sixty days" symbolize as far as time is concerned?

6. The Book of Revelation is written not to lead people to _____ but to _____ .

7. Repentance (in verse 3) is symbolized by the two witnesses being dressed in _____ .

8. If these two witnesses in verse 3 represent Old Testament heroes, they probably are _____ and _____ .

9. The olive trees in verse 4 are the _____ , and the lampstands refer to the _____ .

10. In verse 8, the symbolic words "Sodom" and "Egypt" refer to _____ .

11. What is the meaning of the phrase that in "Sodom" and "Egypt" the Lord was crucified?

12. What does the refusal to bury the witnesses symbolize?

13. What is the horrible message in verse 10?

14. What is the consoling message in verse 11?

15. In verse 13, the tremendous earthquake is a symbol of _____ or _____ upheaval.

16. What does the seventh trumpet announce?

17. In verse 19, when the heavens open what is revealed?

18. What would you say if the Lord were to ask you, "Do you really want to be a true follower of Christ"?

19. Through Baptism you became a member of the Body of Christ. What does that mean to you?

Moment of Prayerful Reflection

1. Read Revelation 11:16-18.
2. Meditate on how the Lord has already rewarded you for the things you have done for him.

Let Us Pray

Lord Jesus, help us to answer your personal call to each of us. Don't let our minds and hearts get cluttered with the evil of the world. Give us insight into your plan and design for our lives. We want to be your true disciples and to re-create your world, with the power of your Holy Spirit, into a world of peace and justice. We need your help! We lift our hearts to you in praise and thanksgiving today and always. Come, Lord Jesus. Amen.

Chapter 13
The Woman and the Dragon
(Revelation 12)

Some of the most bizarre visions of John are contained in this and the following chapter. They are right out of *Star Wars*. They form the core of the entire Book. Their message: The ultimate evil, symbolized by the dragon and the two beasts, contends with the ultimate good, symbolized by the Lamb. The Lamb conquers and will continue to conquer in every age. So, the Book of Revelation is not just reporting what happened 2,000 years ago; it is describing what happens in every age until the Second Coming of the Lord. There will always be the dragon and the two beasts, and there will always be the Lamb who wins every time. This is the universal, timeless message of the Book of Revelation.

Knowing this, we need not waste our time trying to figure out whether Russia (or some other world power) is the dragon and nuclear armaments are the beasts who do the dragon's will. The message remains the same: ''The Lamb is going to win!''

Verse 1: "A great sign appeared in the sky, a woman clothed with the sun, with the moon under her feet, and on her head a crown of twelve stars." The "woman" is a combination of several images to form one solid symbol. Later on (in verse 6), to escape the dragon she flees into the desert. The desert, in symbolic language, is the place we seek to get away from rejection and persecution. The Lord loves those who are persecuted. He cares deeply about them. This woman, then, is a symbol of the suffering Christian community in John's time.

Early Christian writers identified the woman as the Church. Medieval Catholicism identified her as Mary, the Mother of Jesus. But modern scholars returned to the original interpretation that she symbolizes the Christian Church. However, in a symbolic way the woman can also be designated as Mary, especially in view of these words from Vatican II: Mary, the Mother of God "is mother of Christ, and mother of men, and most of all those who believe" (*The Church,* #54). She is the model for all the People of God, and she has been given the title "Mary, Mother of the Church." This makes her the primary model of Christian discipleship.

Verse 2: "Because she was with child, she wailed aloud in pain as she labored to give birth." Although the woman in Revelation symbolizes Mary only in an adapted sense, it is fascinating to compare her to the Virgin of Guadalupe, the Mother of the Americas. She, too, is clothed with the sun, with a crescent moon under her feet, and her garments besprinkled with stars. We can imagine this scene taking place in heaven back in 1531: Jesus tells his Mother to go down to earth and help those people who need assurance very badly. And she might well have said, "I think I'll do Apocalypse 12."

Our Lady of Guadalupe is a perfect "visual aid." The

woman "was with child." In her picture the Virgin of Guadalupe is wearing a maternity belt commonly used by native women at that time. Symbolically, she will give birth to a new people here in the Americas. Around her neck is a small piece of cloth with a cross on it. Her head is bowed and the palms of her hands are pressed together, the fingers pointing up in typical Indian fashion. Her whole attitude seems to be saying, "There is someone greater than I." She is not standing there lording it over others. Her head is bowed in humility. The Virgin of Guadalupe images the characteristics of the people who make up the Church of the Lamb.

Mary's appearance at Guadalupe and the symbolic adaptation that Mary is the woman in Revelation should not deter us from accepting the general consensus of Scripture scholars. Mary cannot be perfectly identified as the woman in Revelation. The woman is the early Christian Church. She is the symbol of the whole Church. "In pain . . . she labored to give birth" to a new age. That message still stands today. The Lamb has won; but we Catholics — like the early Christians — must go through pain and suffering if we are to participate in the victory.

Verses 3,4: "Then another sign appeared . . . a huge dragon . . . with seven heads and ten horns [and] seven diadems." The dragon is the epitome of evil. And, recalling our numerical symbols, if seven signifies fullness, then that number plus three denotes the perfection of fullness. A horn is a symbol of power; ten of them symbolize awesome power. Altogether, then, the dragon has complete sovereignty over evil in the world. But "his tail swept [only] a third of the stars from the sky." With all his power, that is the most he can muster. Who will win between the dragon and the Lamb? Only the Lamb can conquer three-thirds! Evil is always limited by the victorious power of Jesus.

Verse 5: "She gave birth to a son — a boy destined to shepherd all the nations with an iron rod. Her child was caught up to God and to his throne." All scholars agree that this "boy" is Jesus Christ. It recalls the earlier image of the Lamb receiving the scroll from the right hand of the Father.

Verse 6: "The woman herself fled into the desert, where a special place had been prepared for her by God; there she was taken care of for twelve hundred and sixty days." Remember what happened to the Israelites? They were in slavery, and after they gained their freedom where did they find rest and consolation and protection? Out in the desert. So, the desert is a traditional place of refuge for Israel.

Verses 7-9: "Then war broke out in heaven." Michael, the guardian angel of Israel, leads his angels in battle against the dragon. Satan, the dragon, is defeated and cast out of heaven. "Hurled down to earth" with his minions, he still prowls the universe. Christians must still battle against him, but we know that we will win because the Lamb has conquered. If we follow the Lord, while seeking the protection of Michael, we, too, will win the battle.

Verses 10-12: "Then . . . a loud voice in heaven" said:
"Now have salvation and power come,
   the reign of our God and the authority of his Anointed
   One.
For the accuser of our brothers is cast out,
   who night and day accused them before our God.
They defeated him by the blood of the Lamb
   and by the word of their testimony;
   love for life did not deter them from death."
The salvation of the world has been accomplished through the Father who sent his Son to redeem it with his blood.

Christians who imitate the Lamb — by denying themselves even unto death — will triumph as the Lamb triumphed. Next, the hymn concludes with these encouraging words: "So rejoice, you heavens, and you that dwell therein!"

Verse 13: "When the dragon saw that he had been cast down to the earth, he pursued the woman who had given birth to the boy." This is another very interesting passage. Evil (the dragon) tried to vanquish God, but Michael won out. So where, then, does evil turn? Against the Church, against the woman in the desert. It seeks out the woman and pursues her. In the same way, it seeks out you and me in our own weaknesses and pursues us. Satan is determined. He can't win over the Lamb, so he turns to the followers of the Lamb. The woman is the symbol of the followers of the Lamb.

Verse 14: "But the woman was given the wings of a gigantic eagle so that she could fly off to her place in the desert." There she will always be taken care of. Remember the symbolism of the eagle? Swiftness. John is saying that God does not delay in protecting his Church. We, then, when evil tempts us, can say, "Give us wings, O Lord, so we can fly to the desert of your protection." God watches over his faithful ones — those who place their trust in the Lamb.

Verses 15,16: "The serpent, however, spewed a torrent of water out of his mouth to search out the woman and sweep her away. The earth then came to the woman's rescue by opening its mouth and swallowing the [spew]." The serpent (sea monster) continues to seek out the woman to destroy her. The "sea" and "spewing out water" are apocalyptic symbols that represent destructive power. The sea was the source from which the evil one sprang. Land is also evil in apocalyptic literature; but, in this case, John alters its meaning. The land, the desert, becomes the protector of the Church. Perhaps he does so in reference to an ancient tradition which designates the earth as mother. In pagan and in primitive societies, the earth is a symbol of motherhood, warm and life-giving. Not only mother hens protect their young; every mother does.

Verse 17: "Enraged at her escape, the dragon" began to war against the woman's offspring. And who are they? "Those who keep God's commandments and give witness to Jesus." The dragon knew our Christian priorities.

First: Keep God's commandments. Simply put, they are two: Love God and love your neighbor. The Ten Commandments of the Old Law can be reduced to these two. We love God when we adore him only, when we revere his name, and when we keep his day holy. We love our neighbor when we obey and respect our parents and other lawful authority, when we respect human life, when we respect the property of others, and when we observe the laws of sexual morality.

Second: Give witness to Jesus. This second requirement is tremendously important. Being Christian means more than just keeping the commandments. It calls us to witness to our faith. We need to consider this more carefully and relate it to our personal lives. We're not too bad on keeping the commandments, but do we sufficiently witness to the power of Jesus Christ in our lives? As soon as a discussion arises over a problem, we excuse ourselves because "we don't talk religion." We just say, "Well, have you seen this neat self-help book from the supermarket?" To witness to Jesus doesn't mean we have to get up on a soapbox and preach. It means that when people ask us how we survive we look right at them and say, "My faith in the Lord does it. *That* is what helps me survive. I don't depend on drugs; I just depend on Jesus." If we really have that kind of faith in Jesus, we will begin to share it with others.

Review and Discussion

1. The message of chapters 12 and 13 in Revelation is that ultimate evil, symbolized by the _____ and the two _____ , contends with good as symbolized by the _____ .

2. In verse 1, what does the woman symbolize?

3. Why does the Catholic Church connect the symbol of the woman in Revelation 12 with the Blessed Virgin Mary?

4. Actually, though, the woman in Revelation 12 is a symbol of the _____ .

5. What is the symbolic meaning of: "She labored to give birth"?

6. What is the symbolic meaning of the "seven heads," "ten horns," and "seven diadems" which describe the dragon?

7. The "boy" referred to in verse 5 is a direct reference to

   _____ .

8. What is the symbolic meaning of "the desert"?

9. Who is Michael?

10. What act of Christian discipline is called for in verses 10 through 12?

11. Why does the dragon, in verse 13, pursue the woman?

12. In verse 14, the woman was given the wings of a gigantic eagle. What does that symbolize?

13. Verse 15 speaks of the earth saving the woman. What does this mean?

14. The two requirements of Christian living, which verse 17 reveals, are to _____ and to _____ .

15. Sometimes when we feel like we are "in the desert" we discover that the Lord uses that time to reveal his love to us the most. What experiences have you had of this?

16. Reflecting on the inspiration of verse 17, in what ways have you recently witnessed to Jesus in your life?

Moment of Prayerful Reflection

1. Read Revelation 12:5-6.
2. Meditate on the times of your life when you have felt left out and depressed and, having turned to the Lord, found strength and peace.

Let Us Pray

Lord Jesus, you teach us that in our moments of "desert experience" we should turn to your Father for the meaning which such an experience can hold for us. Help us, in the future, to cherish the moments of insight that come from our pain and suffering and to use this insight to help each other and give you praise. We give you our love and praise forever! Come, Lord Jesus. Amen.

Chapter 14
The Two Beasts
(Revelation 13)

In this chapter the dragon delegates two beasts to take over where he left off. The persecution continues under the direction of one beast rising from the sea and one rising from the earth. The first beast is a combination of the four beasts described in chapter 7 of Daniel.

Verse 1: This first beast has "ten horns and seven heads" and "ten diadems on its heads." If people want to say that this beast represents Russia or some other nation, let them. But the 2,000-year tradition of the Catholic Church says that John is writing from a historical context, and the beast is the Roman Empire. The "seven heads" represent the seven emperors of Rome.

Verses 2,3: After a further description of the beast, John says that the dragon bestows on the beast "his own power and throne, together with great authority." Note the direct contrast here with the enthronement of the Lamb as recorded in 5:12.

"I noticed that one of the beast's heads seemed to have been mortally wounded, but this mortal wound was healed." This is a confusing passage whose complete meaning is debated by scholars. It may be referring to Nero, who in A.D. 68 killed himself with a sword and, then, according to legend, came back to life. The legend was false, of course; but during the succeeding years any persecution of Christians by Roman authorities was saddled on Nero. His name became a symbol for Christian persecution. So, whoever headed the Roman Empire during these Christian persecutions is referred to as Nero. This is important to understand because of its relationship with the famous number 666 mentioned later on in this chapter. Thus, according to this interpretation, Nero stands as the personification of the Roman Empire during this period of persecution.

This particular passage may also refer, symbolically, to what happened in Rome after Julius Caesar was assassinated. A rather tumultuous period followed in the wake of Caesar's death. But when Augustus came to the throne he established a Rome greater than that of any ruler before him. Other nations were greatly impressed by this healing of a "mortal wound" inflicted by Brutus but healed by Augustus. Some scholars think that it is this healing restoration that is referred to in this particular passage.

Verses 4-8: People worship both the dragon and the beast. The latter is given authority to blaspheme against God but only for the duration of "forty-two months." The beast has been given authority to wreak evil on the entire world ("every race and people"). Where, then, is the Church during these forty-two months? Remember, that is the length of time the woman was in the desert. So, what is the author saying? During the time the beast has been given the power to inflict evil, the Church is in the "desert" or, in other words, under the protection of God. Only those whose names are written "in the book of the living" will refuse to worship the beast.

Verses 9,10: "Let him who has ears heed these words! If one is destined for captivity, into captivity he goes! If one is destined to be slain by the sword, by the sword he will be slain! Such is the faithful endurance that distinguishes God's holy people." We are called to accept the will of God, no matter what. We know that God will protect the Church, but every Christian must be willing to accept suffering in pursuit of salvation.

Verses 11-13: "Then I saw another wild beast." The first beast came out of the sea. This one comes out of the earth and receives the authority to promote the worship of the first beast throughout the world. Thus, it symbolizes false prophets. We can almost hear them saying to the Christians: "Worship the emperors. Just look at what they have done. They brought the Roman Empire from destruction to full restoration. They must be divine." All this, of course, was in direct opposition to everything the Christians believed.

Verses 14,15: "Because of the prodigies it was allowed to perform by authority of the first beast, it led astray the earth's inhabitants, telling them to make an idol in honor of the beast that had been wounded by the sword and yet lived." The emperor — even his idol — must be worshiped; otherwise, death was in the offing.

Verses 16,17: The second beast now forces all persons to be stamped on the right hand or forehead with the image of the beast. In chapter 7, the Lamb marked the servants of God with a divine seal. Here, the second beast seals people with evil and corruption.

Verse 18: Here we have the strangest verse in the entire Book of Revelation. It begins with a word of caution: "A certain wisdom is needed here." But scarcely anyone has paid any attention to those six words. Interpreters have gone wild trying to explain the enigma. The text then continues, "with a little ingenuity, anyone can calculate the number of the beast, for it is a number that stands for a certain man. The man's number is six hundred sixty-six." Who is this man? Many persons have been suggested; but the most likely candidate is Caesar Nero, the first to persecute the Church in the name of the Roman Empire. How do we arrive at that name? The numerology is complicated but here it is.

In ancient times each letter of the Hebrew alphabet had a numerical symbol assigned to it for various writing purposes. If we take the Hebrew word for Nero Caesar, we have the Hebrew letters N,R,W,N,Q,S,R. Each of those letters has a numerical value: N is 50, R is 200, W is 6, N is 50, Q is 100, S is 60, and R is 200. Now, the numerical equivalents of the name (Nero Caesar) in Hebrew add up to 666.

So, it seems that John is referring to the historical Nero Caesar as a symbol of all the Roman emperors who persecuted the early Christians. But, of course, this passage also refers to the faithful living in today's world. We, too, can expect suffering and persecution as we strive to follow the Lamb.

Review and Discussion

1. In verse 1, what does the beast symbolize?
2. What are the theories about the identity of the beast, one of whose heads seemed to be mortally wounded?
3. Where was the Church during the time when the beast was given authority for only forty-two months?
4. What do verses 9 and 10 call us to do?
5. What does the second beast symbolize?
6. How did the false prophets lead the people astray?

7. How does the number "666" symbolize the Emperor Nero?
8. In what ways do you in your life suffer persecution as you try to follow the way of the Lord Jesus?

Moment of Prayerful Reflection

1. Read Revelation 13:9-10.
2. Meditate on what you feel the will of God is for you at this time of your life.

Let Us Pray

Lord Jesus, we struggle so often to match our will with yours. Give us the insight to accept that whatever you will for us is what will bring us peace and happiness. Help us to perceive, in the daily movements of our lives, what you wish us to do and to be. We are your people. We believe in you and your way. We trust you and your loving care for us. We know that what you desire for us is your heart's desire. May we always be illumined by your divine insight, so that we will always turn to you to discover what is best for our lives. We praise you for your love for us and give you our hearts' adoration and praise forever and ever. Come, Lord Jesus. Amen.

Chapter 15
Reward and Punishment
(Revelation 14)

Once again — lest we become disconsolate on hearing of so much evil heaped on the world — the author of Revelation in the beginning of this chapter writes words of consolation to those who remain faithful to the Lamb.

Verses 1-3: "Then the Lamb appeared . . . standing on Mount Zion." Jerusalem is Mount Zion, and that is where Jewish tradition maintained the faithful would be gathered for the Second Coming. And all those who had been sealed (see chapter 7) were there to meet him. Then, after the usual sounds of thunder indicating God's presence, the faithful all begin to sing a new song to the accompaniment of heavenly harpists. Only the faithful, of course, know the words and follow the tune. Please God, when that day comes for all of us we will be able to say: "They're playing our song."

Verses 4,5: The singers are described as "men who have

never been defiled by immorality with women. They are pure and follow the Lamb wherever he goes.'' Now, what does that mean? It means that they have not fallen into idolatry. Let me explain. Many aspects of pagan religious cults had sexual overtones; their fertility rites centered around re-generation of life. Therefore, in many pagan temples, one of the ways a person united with the divine was to have sexual intercourse with a ''sacred prostitute.'' This is what John is referring to in this passage. These faithful followers had never been defiled by immorality with the sacred prostitutes of the pagan temples. Therefore, they were free of idolatry and dedicated to the Lord.

These verses emphasize the importance of reading Scrip-ture in its true historical context. If we read the above verses out of context, we could conclude that every act of sexual intercourse is tantamount to damnation. We might say, ''The saved ones were never involved with women.'' But that would be a very limiting qualification! That's why we must return to the sources in our study of Scripture.

Verses 6-11: Now that the fate of the faithful is assured, an angel cries out to the entire world: ''Honor God and give him glory. . . . Worship the Creator of heaven and earth.'' This is an invitation for all people to glorify God by worshiping him as their Creator. If they fail to do so, they will be judged and condemned as described in the following verses.

''Fallen, fallen is Babylon [Rome] the great, which made all nations drink the poisoned wine of her lewdness.'' Fallen is any idolatry, any worship of anyone or anything except the one true God.

Now follows a vivid description of what will happen to the damned. God's wrath will be upon them; they will be tormented in burning sulphur forever; and they will have no relief day or night. (Fire-and-brimstone preachers love to expand on this passage.)

Verses 12,13: Here John slips in another word of encouragement to those "who keep the commandments of God and their faith in Jesus." A voice reminds them that the dead who die in the Lord are happy now; and the Spirit adds that they will "find rest from their labors, for their good works accompany them."

Verses 14-16: Now, John anticipates what will happen at the Final Judgment. There appears "One like a Son of Man" wearing a gold crown (indicating a conqueror) and holding a sickle (indicating his role as judge). He wields his sickle and reaps the earth's harvest. Thus he gathers in his faithful ones. They are the harvest wheat.

Verses 17-20: Next, the divine judgment on the unjust is described. An angel cries out: "Use your sharp sickle and gather the grapes from the vines of the earth." So the angel wields his sickle, gathers the grapes, and throws them into the "winepress of God's wrath." "The winepress was trodden outside the city, and so much blood poured out of the winepress that for two hundred miles around, it reached as high as a horse's bridle." The "city" refers to Jerusalem as a symbol of the Church and the fullness of what the Church will be when Jesus comes again. Capital punishment, in ancient times, always took place, by law, outside the city gates. Jesus himself was crucified as a criminal outside the gates of Jerusalem. "Two hundred miles" is symbolic language. Excessive evil brings out exaggerated style among the apocalyptics.

Now, before we begin our next chapter, here is a short review of Revelation's basic message: In *every* age there will always be tension between the dragon and the Lamb. There will always be those who turn to other gods, to evil. There will always be the faithful who are sealed by the Lamb. At times this tension will be feverish. At other times the tension may relax a bit. However, the dragon (evil) will always be limited in what he can do. Thus far in Revelation we have seen that his activities are restricted to a certain fraction. And this is true for all time. He cannot win because the Lamb has won.

Review and Discussion

1. In verse 3, why can only the faithful sing the hymn referred to there?
2. What is the meaning of the phrase (in verse 4) "men who have never been defiled by immorality with women"?
3. In verse 8, Babylon symbolizes _____ .
4. What does the sickle in verse 14 symbolize?
5. Who are the people harvested in verse 16?
6. Who are the people harvested in verse 19?
7. The "city" (in verse 20) is _____ .
8. How would you summarize the basic message of Revelation thus far?
9. If the faithful are the ones who can sing the hymn of praise to the Lord, what hymn could you sing to him for all he has done for you? Describe the blessings you have received from the Lord.
10. What tensions do you feel in your life as you try to follow the Lord?

Moment of Prayerful Reflection

1. Read Revelation 14:13.
2. Meditate on the good works you do in honor of the Lord which bring you interior peace and will bring you to eternal joy.

Let Us Pray

Lord Jesus, day by day we strive to live your way. Through joyous times and difficult moments we place our entire trust in you. When we have moments of joy and

peace we give you our praise and thanks. In difficult moments we turn to you to seek your guidance and your consoling aid. May we always share your message with one another. May the crucifixion you endured remind us that we have no fear if we place ourselves in your loving hands and struggle to overcome evil in our lives. For we know, if we die to sin, we shall rise to glory through your power. We lift our hearts to you in praise and thanksgiving forever. Come, Lord Jesus. Amen.

Chapter 16
The Seven Last Plagues
(Revelation 15,16)

Having just described in vivid detail the harvesting of the just and the unjust, the author of Revelation now turns to a more particularized portrayal of what will happen at that time. Chapters 15 and 16 bring us the last seven plagues.

Revelation 15

Here begin the predictions of the last plagues — showing God's anger in apocalyptic style, his final purging of evil.

Verse 1: "I saw in heaven another sign, great and awe-inspiring: seven angels holding the seven final plagues which would bring God's wrath to a climax." Thus John introduces the seven plagues.

Verses 2-4: After this brief introduction, John calls our attention to the faithful ones — those who will escape these seven plagues. "I then saw something like a sea of glass mingled with fire. On the sea of glass were standing those who had won the victory over the beast and its image." This concept of "glass" separating the divine world from the human world appeared before (in 4:6) — where God gazes from the divine world into the human. "Mingled with fire" probably symbolizes the torture by fire suffered by many of those who had been persecuted and undergone the torment of martyrdom. Also, the concept of fire as sanctifying implies that there will *have* to be a purgation, that there *must* be suffering! The suffering will be sanctifying.

"They sang the song of Moses . . . and the song of the Lamb: 'Mighty and wonderful are your works, LORD God Almighty.' " This song harps back to Moses and his fellow Israelites who sang their song of freedom as they marched toward the Promised Land. It continues in praise of the "King of the nations" who is righteous and true in all his ways. And it concludes by proclaiming that all nations will eventually worship him because his "mighty deeds are clearly seen."

Verses 5-8: Here John returns to the seven plagues. In another vision he sees "the heavenly sanctuary, which is the tent of witness." It opens up and out of it come the seven angels holding the seven plagues. "The angels were dressed in pure white linen, each with a sash of gold about his breast. One of the four living creatures gave to the seven angels seven golden bowls filled with the wrath of the God who lives forever and ever. Then the sanctuary became so filled with the smoke . . . that no one could enter it until the seven plagues . . . had come to an end." The early Christians prayed for strength and courage to face the evil persecution, and their prayers were heard — as is evident from the great number of martyrs among the faithful. But, here, "the smoke" that filled the tent so that "no one could enter" indicates that, no matter how many prayers are said, these plagues will take place.

It should also be noted that these plagues are not limited, as were the other disasters that followed the trumpet blasts. They have a universal character. They will befall the followers of the Anti-Christ, the faithless one; they will touch the unrepentant world at large. Their purpose is to show just how far God will go in his attempt to bring the *entire* world to repentance and to conversion.

Revelation 16

This chapter recounts the plagues that followed after each of the seven bowls were poured out.

Verses 1-3: The angels are told to pour out upon the earth the bowls of God's wrath. The first plague — similar to the sixth one in Egypt — produced "festering boils" to break out among the followers of the beast. The second plague caused the sea to turn to "blood," killing all creatures within it. The "sea," in symbolic language, is the place where evil resides.

Verses 4-7: "The third angel poured out his bowl on the rivers and springs. These also turned to blood." Then an angel is heard to say:
"You are just, O Holy One
    who is and who was,
    in passing this sentence!
To those who shed the blood of saints and prophets,
    you have given blood to drink;
    they deserve it."
This latter sentence echoes the law of the Old Testament: an eye for an eye, a tooth for a tooth. They shed the blood; therefore, the blood will be upon them. The faithful are vindicated and rejoice in their vindication.

Verses 8,9: The sun is the recipient of the contents of the fourth bowl. The angel was "commissioned to burn men with fire. Those who were scorched by the intense heat blasphemed the name of God." They still didn't repent. They still didn't change! They wouldn't listen! These verses contain a basic Christian theme — one told in Scripture from the beginning of the Book of Genesis to the final verse of Revelation. God constantly invites and urges people to change and live according to his plan and his way. When something good happens to them, they ignore him. When something bad happens, they blaspheme him.

Verses 10,11: "The fifth angel poured out his bowl on the throne of the beast. Its kingdom was plunged into darkness." This "throne" symbolizes the force of evil (the Roman Empire). And because of their suffering, men "blasphemed the God of heaven. . . . But they did not turn away from their wicked deeds."

Verses 12-16: The sixth angel poured out his bowl on the great river Euphrates. Its water was dried up to prepare the way for the kings of the East. The Parthians resided on the Euphrates. Their powerful kings are the ones referred to here. Then three unclean spirits "who worked prodigies" gathered "the kings of the earth for battle on the great day of God the Almighty." And the place where they assembled them is called in Hebrew, "Armageddon." This word is presumed to mean "the mound of Megiddo." In Jewish history some of the most decisive Jewish battles took place at the pass near Megiddo. So, here Armageddon is a symbol of a decisive routing of the forces of evil.

Verses 17-21: "Finally, the seventh angel poured out his bowl upon the empty air. From the throne in the sanctuary came a loud voice which said, 'It is finished!' " Obviously, the voice is that of God proclaiming to the world that these are the last warnings he will send and that everything is over. With this announcement, there took place the greatest display of thunder and lightning — followed by a violent earthquake — that this world has ever seen. Finally, "the great city [Rome] was split into three parts, and the other Gentile cities also fell." In 11:13 only one-tenth of the city was destroyed. Here, "split into three parts" indicates that Rome will be totally and completely destroyed. The final verses show that despite the severity of all these plagues men refuse to accept these warnings and continue to blaspheme God.

Review and Discussion

Revelation 15

1. This chapter predicts the _____ .
2. Verse 2 mentions a sea of glass mingled with fire. What does this symbolize?
3. The "Song of Moses" appears in verse 3. In your own words, write your own song of freedom.
4. In verse 8, what is the symbolic meaning of the words "no one could enter"?

Revelation 16

5. What is the purpose of the seven bowls in this chapter?
6. In verse 3, what does the sea symbolize?
7. How are the martyrs vindicated in verses 4 through 7?
8. What is the basic Christian theme indicated in the commentary under verses 8 and 9?
9. The "throne of the beast" (in verse 10) refers to ____

   _____ .
10. Who are "kings from the East" in verse 12?
11. What does "Armageddon" refer to in verse 16?

12. What is the message contained in verse 17?
13. In verse 19, the great city is "split into three parts." What does this mean?
14. What do you do in your daily life to curb evil in our times?
15. What does the fact that Jesus is the Lord of creation and the Victor over all evil mean to you personally?

Moment of Prayerful Reflection

1. Read Revelation 15:3-4.
2. Meditate on the mighty and wonderful works that the Lord has done in your life.

Let Us Pray

Lord Jesus, we give you honor and praise for all you have done in the history of time to share with us the plan of your Father. You teach us through your way to be ambassadors of brotherhood/sisterhood and peace and reconciliation. In our moments of struggle give us the insight to turn to you and to be inspired by your example. May we spend our days fostering your Kingdom of love and forgiveness to all. We give you praise and glory forever. Come, Lord Jesus. Amen.

Chapter 17
Babylon, Symbol of Abomination
(Revelation 17)

In this chapter and the following one we finally come to the fall of Babylon, referred to twice previously (14:8 and 16:19) in Revelation. Here we have John's vision of the great city and the interpretation of the vision. The symbols that the author uses in these passages are "deliberately obscure," so we should not be too quick to say that *this* and not *that* is the one and only interpretation of a given symbol.

Although Babylon obviously refers to Rome, for the Israelites the city by the Euphrates was already an abomination in their memories. It was there that they were held captive for so many years; and after they returned to Jerusalem they were never really an independent nation again. So, Babylon — for them — symbolized persecution. In John's time, therefore — when Roman authorities began and continued to persecute the Christians — it was easy for the Christian community to recognize that "Babylon" meant "Rome."

Verses 1,2: "Then one of the seven angels . . . came to me and said: 'Come, I will show you the judgment in store for the great harlot who sits by the waters of the deep.' " The "deep" is a place of evil. "The kings of the earth have committed fornication with her, and the earth's inhabitants have grown drunk on the wine of her lewdness." Pagan nations conquered by Rome have accepted the cult of emperors.

Verses 3,4: "The angel then carried me away in spirit to a desolate place where I saw a woman seated on a scarlet beast which was covered with blasphemous names. This beast had seven heads [great knowledge] and ten horns [tremendous power]." This "desolate place" or wilderness contrasts with the "desert" where the woman in chapter 12 took refuge from the dragon. The harlot (Rome) resides in the wilderness; the woman (the Church) lives in the desert where she is protected. The harlot sits on the beast which is the symbol of evil on the earth. This is the beast described in chapter 13:1-9.

Rome, therefore, as symbolized by the harlot, is intimately connected with evil. And the evil is the imperial cult demanding worship of the emperor. A further indication that the harlot is Rome is contained in the description of her dress: "purple and scarlet," "gold and pearls and other jewels" — all the trappings of imperial splendor and power.

Verses 5,6: "On her forehead was written a symbolic name, 'Babylon the great, mother of harlots and all the world's abominations.' " It was a custom in the Roman Empire — particularly in the city of Rome — for prostitutes to identify themselves by having their names painted on their foreheads. This verse may be alluding to that custom. The woman who "was drunk with the blood of God's holy ones and the blood of those martyred for their faith in Jesus'' refers to Rome as the persecutor of the early Christian martyrs.

John is shocked on seeing all this evil — even though the angel had forewarned him and Jesus had assured him that he would win out in the end. Perhaps — in a lesser degree — we can compare it to the way we feel when we see on television the results of a riot, the consequences of drug abuse, the horror of mass murder. We say to ourselves, ''That's unbelievable.'' John must have felt somewhat the same way about this vision of abominations.

Verses 7,8: Here we begin the interpretation of the vision. The angel says: ''I will explain to you the symbolism of the woman and of the seven-headed and ten-horned beast carrying her. The beast you saw existed once but now exists no longer. It will come up from the abyss once more before going to final ruin.'' Although there are other explanations of this passage, some scholars maintain that the beast is a personification of the emperor Nero. Nero, who had existed, no longer exists; but he will exist again in the continuation of the emperors. This was especially true during the reign of Domitian. The pagan cult of the emperor's divinity was so strong at that time that people began to look upon succeeding emperors as reincarnations of Nero.

So, Domitian was, at the time of John, the reincarnation of Nero. ''He did exist. He doesn't exist. He will exist again.'' This is an apocalyptic play on words. It refers to Nero not as a person *per se,* but as a symbol of imperial authority and power which at that time was persecuting the early Christian community.

Verses 9,10: ''Here is the clue for one who possesses wisdom! The seven heads are seven hills on which the woman sits enthroned. They are also seven kings: five have already fallen, one lives now, and the last has not yet come;

but when he does come he will remain only a short while.'' The seven hills refer to Rome, which is built on seven hills. The ''seven kings'' and the ''five already fallen'' are allusions to the series of emperors between the time of Nero and Domitian. (It is thought that John wrote his Book during the reign of Domitian [A.D. 81-96].) John uses an ambiguous style to refer to this period in Rome's history. Always, Babylon is Rome, and the harlot is a personification of Rome. If we keep these facts in mind, everything falls into place, no matter what the imagery.

Verses 11-14: ''The beast which existed once but now exists no longer, even though it is an eighth king, is really one of the seven and is on its way to ruin.'' This refers to Domitian. He is the eighth emperor in the line of Nero, but eight does not fit the earlier symbolism of seven. So, John has to explain here why eight is actually seven. Confusing, isn't it? But, no matter — after declaring that ten other kings will join the beast in destroying Rome (verses 12 and 13), John reverts to his original message: ''They will fight against the Lamb but the Lamb will conquer them, for he is the Lord of lords and the King of kings; victorious, too, will be his followers — the ones who were called: the chosen and the faithful.''

The evil world will fight against the Lamb. But he will conquer, and his faithful followers will celebrate victory with him. This is the recurring theme of the Book of Revelation. It is not a horror story about what is going to happen in the twentieth or twenty-first or ninety-first century. Revelation is a very simple book, really. It has a very specific theme: The world is evil; it gets worse day by day. God permits evil to exist. In the end, Jesus, who is Lord of lords and King of kings, will win and his followers will win with him. They will be victorious. So, rather than be afraid of what's going to happen we should just join Jesus in the fight against evil. As his followers we will be victorious.

Verses 15-18: "The angel then said to me: 'The waters on which you saw the harlot enthroned are large numbers of peoples and nations and tongues.'" This refers to the populace of the entire Roman Empire. "The ten horns [power] you saw on the beast will turn against the harlot with hatred; they will strip off her finery and leave her naked; they will devour her flesh and set her on fire." Other nations, as indicated in verse 13, now join the beast and help to destroy evil Rome — unwittingly carrying out God's "plan."

Review and Discussion

1. Even before Revelation was written, what was Israel's attitude toward Babylon?
2. How does the woman seated on the beast in verse 3 differ from the woman in chapter 12?
3. What is the contrast between the "desolate place" in verse 3 and the "desert" in chapter 12?
4. In verses 3 and 4, why is the woman dressed so expensively?
5. In verse 5, what is a possible explanation of the word "Babylon" written on the forehead of the woman seated on the beast?
6. Why is John astonished (in verse 7) at what he sees?
7. In verse 8, what is the meaning of "the beast you saw existed once but now exists no longer"?
8. In verse 9, where are the seven hills located?
9. Why is verse 14 a summary of the entire message of Revelation?
10. In verse 17, who helps the beast to destroy evil Rome?
11. What abominations of present society do we need to war against with the power of the Lord?
12. Why do you think God permits evil to exist?

Moment of Prayerful Reflection

1. Read Revelation 17:14.
2. Meditate on how you need to put your life into the hands of the victorious Lord so as to overcome the evil in your life.

Let Us Pray

Lord Jesus, we thank you for calling us to be in solidarity with you and your risen power. Help us daily to perceive how you are always victorious over evil and how all we need to do is place our trust in your victory and love for us. Inspired by this trust, may we join hands with you in fighting the injustice and evil of our times. May we never depend solely on our own resources but open our hearts to your power. May our endeavors to re-create a better world receive your blessing. We praise you as we offer you our devotion and fidelity. Come, Lord Jesus. Amen.

Chapter 18
Fall of Babylon
(Revelation 18)

Having just seen — in the last chapter — the vision of the judgment of Babylon (Rome) and the interpretation of that vision, we now view its fall through the eyes of those who profited most from its iniquities. These scenes are presented in a series of lamentations.

We should remind ourselves that John is not predicting the rise and fall of the Roman Empire. He is not writing a history book. He is using Rome as a symbol. We all have a Rome in our hearts. Revelation is written from this perspective. It is as if John is saying, "Look first to see the harlot's symbol in your own life and how closely you are attached to the beast of evil in the world." Thus, Revelation contains a universal lesson for the Church and also a personal lesson for each one of us.

Verses 1-3: An angel whose "authority was so great that all the earth was lighted up by his glory" begins the first lamentation:

"Fallen, fallen is Babylon the great!
    She has become a dwelling place for demons. . . .
For she has made all the nations drink
    the poisoned wine of her lewdness [idolatry].
The kings of the earth committed fornication [practiced
    idolatry] with her,
    and the world's merchants grew rich from her wealth
    and wantonness."
The kings and the merchants are sad with good reason.

Verses 4-8: These verses contain a warning to the elect:
"Depart from her, my people,
    for fear of sinning with her
    and sharing the plagues inflicted on her!"
They should leave Rome and follow the Lamb.
    Verse seven reveals one of the key sins of Rome.
"In proportion to her boasting and sensuality,
    repay her in torment and grief!
For she said to herself,
    'I sit enthroned as a queen.
No widow am I,
    and never will I go into mourning!' "
Jesus, however, tells his followers: "Blest . . . are the
sorrowing; they shall be consoled" (Matthew 5:4). "Blest
are the lowly; they shall inherit the land" (Matthew 5:5). The
key sin here seems to be imperial arrogance: "We are the
end-all of creation. Our laws are divine. Our emperor is God.
We are not answerable to any higher authority." But God
says, "Yes, you *are* answerable to a higher authority. You are
not the end-all. You are my people. You are subject to the
divine laws that I have instituted for the universe."

When we commit sin we do something similar. We make
ourselves unanswerable to a higher authority. God says,
"Thou shalt not steal." We ignore his law; and we steal.
Who, then, is the lawgiver? Not God, obviously. We do only

what we want to do. What we are saying is this: "We're not going to listen to anybody, including you, Lord."

Babylon (Rome) represents evil — that evil which began with Adam and Eve. God said: "Do this." And they answered: "We'll do what we want to do." And they did. So, here, Rome is saying, "I want nothing but my own pleasure, and I will allow no suffering in my life." But the Lamb says just the opposite. "I came to suffer; I came to serve. And I call you to follow me." What a complete contrast between Babylon, the harlot, and Jesus, the Lamb.

All this, of course, has ramifications for our own personal lives. How often we say to someone who irritates us, "Get out of my life!" Why? Not because we can't tolerate him or her — because we might be able to do that — but because we're not in the mood, and we want to be happy right now! We want nothing to do with mourning or suffering or obeying. So, there is a very personal message here for us; and we need to reflect on it frequently.

I stress this because the Book of Revelation is not meant to be read like we would read a book on the early history of the Church. That's not what it's all about. Revelation is a book of personal inspiration, relying on catastrophical symbols of the universe to attract our attention. Its chief meaning for us will depend on the way that we see all these symbols within ourselves, as well as in society around us and in the world.

Verses 9-19: These next eleven verses describe the reactions to the fall of Babylon (Rome) as seen through the eyes of three groups who prospered most because of their submission to this great city. They are the kings, the merchants, and the seafaring men. This entire passage spells out, in apocalyptic language, how they all participated in the evil which is now being lamented. Each group reacts in the same way: They "keep their distance for fear of the punishment inflicted on her [Babylon]." They had put all their trust in the purple-robed harlot seated on the beast. They had subjugated themselves to the Roman Empire, and now Rome is crumbling beneath its ponderous evil.

The Book of Revelation indicates that punishment for our sins comes not from God but is built into our evil actions. We punish ourselves. We tell one lie, and that leads to another and still another. God doesn't make us feel nervous and guilty; we feel that way all by ourselves.

This is also true of anger and hatred. In an unchristian moment we begin to hate someone. And that person, unchristianly, hates us in return. Our punishment for hatred given is hatred received. Of course, for every act — whether good or bad — there is a reaction. Sometimes, too, a good act will provoke a bad reaction, and vice versa.

Parents follow this line of thinking — to a degree — when they tell their children that if they do the right thing they will be rewarded; but if they do the wrong thing they can expect punishment. I saw an example of this recently while visiting a friend of mine. Joe has a little boy named Joey, who, at that time, was about three. We were eating dinner, and Joey's little sister, who was about seven, came in to say, "I was watching TV and Joey came and changed the channel." Joe said, "Well, tell Joey to come in here." So in came Joey. He stood there, and his dad looked at him and said, "Well, did you?" And he said, "Yes." "Did you think about it?" Joey answered, "Yes." Joe then asked him, "What are you going to do now?" Joey responded, "I'm going to go to my room and stay there until you tell me I can come out." Joe said, "Bye." Joey, looking like he had been run over by a Mack truck, said, "Bye." And off he went to his room. Joe explained to me, "A long time ago we told the kids that when they do anything they should be ready to accept the consequences. So, we told them to think before they acted — because there will always be a consequence." That's right out of Revelation!

Joe then related a cute story. He said they have another household rule: Before bedtime each night everything must be picked up around the house and put in its proper place. Otherwise, it goes into this big box in the hallway and stays there for a week. Regardless of what it is, that's where it goes. So everybody scurries around at the end of the evening before going to bed, putting away all the toys and anything else left lying around. Then, at bedtime, if something is still out of place, it goes into the big box. One evening Joe went into his study to answer the telephone. He was very tired. So, after he had hung up the phone, he kicked off his shoes, leaned back in his chair, and fell asleep. Now just before bedtime, Joey went into the study, picked up his father's shoes, and put them in the big box in the hallway. Then Joey waited to see what would happen. Well, those shoes were the only really good pair that Joe owned. So, later he told his wife, ''I've got to have those shoes.'' ''Not on your life,'' she retorted. ''They stay in there.'' ''But I didn't really go to bed.'' ''That's what the kids say. Forget it! The shoes stay in there for a week.''

Verses 20-24: After words of encouragement to the ''saints, apostles and prophets,'' an angel ''picked up a stone like a huge millstone and hurled it into the sea and said: 'Babylon the great city shall be cast down like this, with violence, and nevermore be found!' '' The symbolism is perfectly clear: Babylon (Rome) will be completely swallowed up. The final verses further emphasize the complete disappearance of the great city from the face of the earth.

Review and Discussion

1. In this chapter, John uses the fall of Babylon as a symbol of _____ .
2. What warning does the early Christian community receive in verse 4?

3. What is one of the key sins of Rome described in verse 7?
4. Who are the three groups (in verses 9, 11, 17) that prospered from the wickedness of Rome?
   1) _____ .
   2) _____ .
   3) _____ .
5. In verse 21, Babylon is cast into the sea like a huge millstone. What does this symbolize?
6. Does God punish us or do we punish ourselves?
7. How is Revelation a book of personal inspiration for you?
8. What is meant by the idea that the punishment of sin is built into the very act of the sin itself?

Moment of Prayerful Reflection

1. Read Revelation 18:14.
2. Meditate on how worthless is any craving for the things of this world. Examine those things which really bring you peace and inner joy.

Let Us Pray

Lord Jesus, so often we turn from you and your teachings and run after the illusions of happiness that our world offers. Afterward, we feel deep isolation and loneliness. Aid us to perceive always that we will only find peace and joy if we follow your way of love, compassion, selfless giving, and forgiveness. May we be messengers of this true peace to all around us. May our actions and words proclaim to all our trust in your way above that of the world. We give you thanks and praise forever. Come, Lord Jesus. Amen.

Chapter 19
Wedding Feast of the Lamb
(Revelation 19)

We now approach the climax of Revelation. The actual judgment scene is preceded by two songs of victory anticipating the final coming of Christ. The first song is sung by the angels, and the second is sung by the entire Church. Then follows a description of Christ's triumph over the power of evil.

Verses 1-4: A great assembly in heaven began to sing:
    "Alleluia!
Salvation, glory and might belong to our God,
    for his judgments are true and just!
He has condemned the great harlot
    who corrupted the earth with her harlotry.
He has avenged the blood of his servants
    which was shed by her hand.''
Justice is the keynote of this song of the angels. At its

conclusion the entire assembly worships God by singing "Amen! Alleluia!" which means "So be it! Praise the Lord!"

Verses 5-8: Next, a voice from the throne bids all the faithful on earth to sing out:
"Alleluia!
The Lord is king. . . .
Let us rejoice and be glad,
  and give him glory!"
Why all this celebration? Because the Kingdom of God is about to begin. "For this is the wedding day of the Lamb; his bride . . . has been given a dress . . . of finest linen, brilliant white."

That God is wedded to his people is expressed in the Old Testament (see Hosea 2:1-23; Isaiah 54:4-8; Ezekiel 16:7f) and in the New Testament (see especially Matthew 22:1-14). And the entire book of The Song of Songs portrays in a sublime manner the mutual love between the Lord and his people. Here in Revelation we have the same type of imagery: As Israel is the bride of Yahweh, so Christ the Lamb is the bride of the Church. The dress which the bride wears, as John himself notes, symbolizes "the virtuous deeds of God's saints." Its simple white linen serves as a striking contrast to "the glittering purple garments of the harlot" described in chapters 17 and 18.

Verses 9,10: After the angel remarks how happy are those "who have been invited to the wedding feast of the Lamb," he tells John that "these words [revelations] are true; they come from God." On hearing this, John falls down in worship at the feet of the angel; but he is told he (the angel) is not God, who alone deserves worship. He is "a fellow servant" — like John and the rest of the faithful — who gives "witness to Jesus."

John's reaction is an interesting commentary on human nature. He was so overwhelmed by what he had seen — the horrendous destruction predicted for the fall of Babylon and now the massive choirs singing the praises of God and celebrating a momentous wedding feast — that he mistook the messenger of God for God himself. We learn from him that modern science, for example, is not God; there is only one God, the Creator of the universe which science itself probes.

Verses 11-16: These verses describe the One who defeats the forces of evil. He rides on a white horse, and he comes as judge and warrior. "His eyes blazed like fire, and on his head were many diadems [supreme power and authority]. Inscribed on his person was a name known to no one but himself."

To "name" someone is to define who or what that person is. That no one but the rider knows the name means that it is incomprehensible to the human mind. On Mount Sinai, Moses asked the Lord his name, and he replied, "Yahweh," which some scholars interpret as "I Am Who I Am." In ancient times, the gods received their names from the people who created them. If they were a warring nation, they named their god Mars. Thus the gods were personifications of the national spirit of the people who named them. The whole process of naming indicates power over the object named, as Adam did with the animals in the Garden. At Sinai, then, God is saying, "You need not know my name. For if you think you know my name, you will presume that you have power over me. But you don't have any power over me. I have power over *you!*" So, the rider has a name that is written on his person, but no one knows it but himself. We know from the context, of course, that the rider is Jesus Christ who controls us. He has called *us* by name. He has sealed *us* with his seal. We don't seal him with ours.

The next few verses describe the rider in his role of warrior, leading "the armies of heaven" against the forces of evil. The "sharp sword" which he uses is the Word of God. He "will tread out in the winepress the blazing wrath of God." He will destroy God's enemies. Now the rider is further identified; on his cloak these words are written: "King of kings and Lord of lords." This is in direct contrast to the beast (see 17:3). On the rider's cloak he has only one title. But the beast has blasphemous names written all over its body. Why? To deceive. "If I can't deceive you with this name, I will deceive you with another. If I can't make you angry, I will make you envious. If I can't make you envious, I will make you jealous." That's the way the beast (devil) proceeds. But Jesus has only one title: Victor. "I am not here to deceive you. I am here to tell you that I have won; and so will you if you follow me."

Verses 17-21: "Next I saw an angel standing on the sun. He cried out in a loud voice to all the birds flying in midheaven: 'Come! Gather together for the great feast God has prepared for you! You are to eat the flesh of kings, of commanders and warriors, of horses and their riders; the flesh of all men, the free and the slave, the small and the great.' " This gruesome scene anticipates the feast — in contrast to the wedding feast — the birds of prey will have after the final massacre described in the following verses. This will be the final battle before the final triumph. The "beast," along with the "false prophet," was captured and "hurled down alive into the fiery pool of burning sulphur," and "the rest were slain by the sword which came out of the mouth of the One who rode the horse."

At this point, no doubt, John presumes that we will swing back to the opening passage, to sing with the angels their song of victory and to celebrate with the Church the wedding feast of the Lamb. The reign of God has begun.

Review and Discussion

1. What is the keynote of the song of the angels recorded in verses 1-3?
2. In verse 7, the bride of the Lamb is _____.
3. What does "the linen dress" in verse 8 symbolize?
4. What important teaching does verse 10 contain?
5. To "name" someone or something has a special meaning. Discuss this in your group.
6. How does the rider's title (in verse 16) contrast with the titles of the beast?
7. What is there about you that makes the Lord delighted in your fidelity to him?
8. How can your acceptance of Jesus as the "King of kings" aid you in the way you live your life?
9. Reread verse 5. Now praise God in your own words.

Moment of Prayerful Reflection

1. Read Revelation 19:6-8.
2. Meditate on the beauty of the calling you have to be the bride of the Lord.

Let Us Pray

Lord Jesus, we give you love, honor, adoration, and praise for calling us to share intimately your love and protection. We celebrate our union with you that fills us with such meaning, power, and security. Help us to announce to all the world the beauty of our union with you. May we clothe ourselves daily with virtuous living, so as to present ourselves always to you as devoted and loving disciples. Keep us from harm and surround us with your love. We praise you as the King of the entire universe and of our personal hearts. Come, Lord Jesus. Amen.

Chapter 20
The Thousand-Year Reign
(Revelation 20)

The first part of this chapter deals with the millenium or the thousand-year reign of Christ, during which Satan will be bound. This topic has intrigued scholars for centuries and is still a popular subject with modern neoapocalyptic writers. The second part describes the Last Judgment.

Verses 1-3: "Then I saw an angel come down from heaven, holding the key to the abyss and a huge chain in his hand. He seized the dragon, the ancient serpent, who is the devil or Satan, and chained him up for a thousand years. The angel hurled him into the abyss which he closed and sealed over him. He did this so that the dragon might not lead the nations astray until the thousand years are over. After this, the dragon is to be released for a short time."

Some early Christian writers understood this passage to mean that Christ will reign with his martyrs for one thousand years in preparation for the founding of the new world. But ever since the time of Saint Augustine (354-430), the Church has accepted his interpretation: The thousand-year reign is symbolic. It signifies a long, indefinite time, extending from Christ's death and Resurrection to his Second Coming — whenever it happens. It will be followed by a short period of persecution. The devil will be bound during this long period of time, but that does not mean that he cannot exert his evil influence. It means that he cannot win. We see this in our own lives. The devil may tempt us, but he cannot win over us unless we freely give him that power over us. Here, however, John is referring to the fact that Satan, who represents the forces of evil, cannot triumph over God, who represents everything that is good.

Verses 4-6: Now John sees the "thrones" of those who will "pass judgment." He also sees "the spirits" of the martyrs. "They came to life again and reigned with Christ for a thousand years." Next, we have this statement: "The others who were dead did not come to life till the thousand years were over. This is the first resurrection. . . . The second death will have no claim on them; they . . . shall reign with him [Christ] for a thousand years." What is meant by the "first resurrection" and the "second resurrection" and the "first death" and the "second death"? Saint Paul refers to these concepts — in their figurative sense — when he writes (in Romans 6:1-8) about Baptism. The first death is sin. The first resurrection is Baptism. When we are baptized we die to sin with Christ and we rise with Christ. The second resurrection refers to justification at the Second Coming of Jesus Christ. The second death is total and absolute damnation at the time of the Second Coming. Those who have been baptized and have followed the Lamb faithfully will not have to suffer the second death. They will welcome the second resurrection at the Second Coming of Jesus. Now, what is the meaning of the verse, "The others who were dead did not come to life until the thousand years were over"? These were the unbaptized. They did not have a first resurrection. They did not come to life until the Second Coming of Jesus.

Verses 7-10: These verses describe what happened when Satan was freed from his prison as the thousand years came to an end. He tries to "seduce" the whole world with the aid of troops from Gog and Magog — symbolic names of Israelite enemies of old. They invade the beloved city (Jerusalem) but are devoured by fire from heaven. And so the devil is cast into hell.

Verses 11-15: Here we finally reach the Last Judgment. "The One who sat on it" [the throne], passes judgment on the entire world. Open is "the book of the living." Each person is judged according to his or her conduct! Those whose names are in "the book of the living" receive their eternal reward, and these whose names are not recorded there go into eternal punishment.

Review and Discussion

1. How does the Church interpret the thousand-year reign mentioned in verse 2?
2. According to verse 2, Satan is chained up for a thousand years. What does this mean?
3. Give the figurative meaning of the following:
   1) "First resurrection" refers to _____ .
   2) "Second resurrection" refers to _____ .
   3) "First death" refers to _____ .
   4) "Second death" refers to _____ .
4. In verse 8, the names "Gog" and "Magog" symbolize
   _____ .
5. Reread verses 11 through 15 and then summarize in your own words their hopeful message.

6. How does the Lord help you to thwart the devil in your own life?
7. At Baptism we die to _____
   and we rise _____ .
8. How will God judge you on Judgment Day?

Moment of Prayerful Reflection

1. Read Revelation 20:12.
2. Meditate on your personal actions and attitudes and reflect on how the Lord will judge them.

Let Us Pray

Lord Jesus, we stand before your judgment every day. Only by your mercy and forgiveness do we rate your salvation. May each day of our lives be spent doing the things that will bring your love into our hearts. May we never do anything which deters the establishment of your reign on earth. May we so live as to deserve your trust in us. We give you praise and honor every day of our lives. Come, Lord Jesus. Amen.

*"He carried me away in spirit to the top
of a very high mountain and showed me the holy city
Jerusalem coming down out of heaven from God."*

(Revelation 21:10)

PART THREE

THE CHURCH TRANSFIGURED

(Revelation 21,22)

OF THE NEW JERUSALEM

Chapter 21
The New Heaven and the New Earth
(Revelation 21)

Now that we have witnessed John's vision of the thousand-year reign, the final defeat of Satan, and the Last Judgment of the just and the unjust, the author describes in this chapter what the eternal Kingdom of God will be like. There will be a new heaven and a new earth.

Verse 1: The created world as we know it will disappear, and a new universe will be fashioned for the faithful ones. ''Then I saw new heavens and a new earth. The former heavens and the former earth had passed away, and the sea [evil] was no longer.'' So, when this world comes to an end, Jesus will create a new world, a place more suitable for those who have been redeemed. (The world in which we presently live was created to fit the needs of fallen humanity.)

Verse 2: ''I also saw a new Jerusalem, the holy city, coming down out of heaven from God, beautiful as a bride prepared to meet her husband.'' This ''new Jerusalem'' comes from the hand of God. She, the bride of Christ — Mother Church — takes up her abode in the new creation.

Verses 3,4: Then a loud voice cries out: "This is God's dwelling among men. . . . They shall be his people and he shall be their God who is always with them. . . . He shall wipe every tear from their eyes, and there shall be no more death or mourning, crying out or pain." God has always cared for his people in the past; but in this new Jerusalem he will dwell with them forever, bestowing on them eternal happiness.

Verse 5: "The One who sat on the throne said to me, 'See, I make all things new!' " This verse is significant because it is the only time in all of Revelation that God himself speaks to John. And he assures him that everything revealed about this new creation, this new and holy city, is absolutely true.

Verse 6: After giving his references, as it were ("I am the Alpha and the Omega"), God then says to John: "To anyone who thirsts I will give to drink without cost from the spring of life-giving water." This is a very consoling message not only to Christians but to all the people of the world. "Anyone" may come to him. God's salvation is open to men and women throughout the entire universe.

Verses 7,8: These verses remind the faithful that they will inherit the gifts mentioned here and warn the unfaithful of the punishment that awaits them.

Verses 9-14: "One of the seven angels who held the seven bowls filled with the seven last plagues came and said to me, 'Come, I will show you the woman who is the bride of the Lamb.' " The "woman," as in verse 2, is the Church. The bride represents the redeemed people. So, John is carried away to a high mountain and is shown the new Jerusalem. The woman and the city are identical: both represent the Church, the People of God.

The next four verses in this passage begin the symbolic description of the holy city. It had "the radiance of a precious jewel." Its walls had "twelve gates" at which "twelve angels" stood. "Twelve names" were inscribed in its gates. Three gates each faced all four directions. And the wall of the city was built on "twelve courses" of stone.

The consistent use of the number "twelve" in this passage points clearly to the twelve tribes of Israel and the twelve apostles. In the new creation there will be no distinction between the Old Testament and the New Testament. All faithful members of both covenants will be part of the great city Jerusalem. They are all the elect and the chosen ones of the Lord.

Verses 15-21: This passage continues to describe the holy city. Again we have more variations of the symbolic number twelve and mention of various stones and precious metals. From these descriptions come some of the expressions that people use in speaking about heaven — such phrases as "the pearly gates" and "the streets of heaven are paved with gold." However, lest we get carried away with these symbols depicted in human language we should keep in mind Paul's description of heaven: "Eye has not seen, ear has not heard, nor has it so much as dawned on man what God has prepared for those who love him" (1 Corinthians 2:9).

Verses 22-27: "I saw no temple in the city. The Lord, God the Almighty, is its temple — he and the Lamb." In ancient Israel, the center of religious worship was the temple in Jerusalem. The Ark of the Covenant was the symbol of God's presence in the midst of the Israelites. There is no need for a temple in the New Jerusalem because Christ is present in each and every member of his Church. And the other symbols in these verses — "no need of sun or moon," for example — further emphasize Christ's presence among the People of God. The glory of God is its light and the Lamb is its lamp. "During the day its gates shall never be shut, and there shall be no night." There is no need for locked doors because "only those shall enter whose names are inscribed in the book of the living kept by the Lamb." And there will be "no night" because Christ, the Light of the world, will shine there eternally.

Review and Discussion

1. What will happen to the created world at the end of time?
2. Who is "the bride of the Lamb" referred to in verse 9?
3. The new Jerusalem described in verses 10-14 symbolizes _____ .
4. In verse 13, what do the three gates facing each point of the compass symbolize?
5. The walls of the city are built on twelve courses of stone (see verse 14). What does this symbolize?
6. In the new creation there will be no distinction between the _____ and the _____ .
7. Are the streets of heaven really paved with gold?
8. Why is there no temple in the new city?
9. How is Christ present in his Church?
10. If you could re-create the world right now, what characteristics would it have?
11. What can you do in your life today to help establish the kind of unity among people that is characteristic of what the Lord desires?

Moment of Prayerful Reflection

1. Read Revelation 21:5-7.
2. Meditate on how wonderful these promising words of the Savior sound to you as his disciple.

Let Us Pray

Lord Jesus, we pray that we might join hands with you each day in making all things new. May we come to you and drink of your living and refreshing water. Invigorated by your love, may we go forth to win over the world to your divine way. We humbly and thankfully acknowledge you as our Lord and Savior. Assist us always with your wisdom and strength. We are your people, dedicated to spreading your message far and wide. We give you our love and praise each day of our lives. Come, Lord Jesus. Amen.

Chapter 22
The River of Life and Testimony of Jesus
(Revelation 22)

This concluding chapter of Revelation contains a further description of the heavenly Jerusalem, followed by a series of warnings and exhortations.

Verses 1-5: "The angel then showed me the river of life-giving water, clear as crystal, which issued from the throne of God and of the Lamb and flowed down the middle of the streets. On either side of the river grew the trees of life which produce fruit twelve times a year, once each month; their leaves serve as medicine for the nations. Nothing deserving a curse shall be found there. The throne of God and of the Lamb shall be there, and his servants shall serve him faithfully. They shall see him face to face and bear his name on their foreheads. The night shall be no more. They will need no light from lamps or the sun, for the Lord God shall give them light, and they shall reign forever."

"Life-giving waters": These will constantly flow in the new Jerusalem. Jesus himself spoke of this in his conversation with the Samaritan woman (see John 4:10-14). On earth this living water comes to us as grace, flowing from our celebration of the sacraments. In heaven it will become part and parcel of our very existence.

"Trees of life": In the Book of Genesis, there is only one tree of life. Now there is a superabundance of trees — trees that produce fruit all the time and for everyone! All this symbolizes an abundance of life.

"Face to face": Even Moses never saw God's face, but those in heaven will see him as he is.

"Need no light": God is their light, and they will reign forever.

Verses 6-10: Here we begin the Epilogue. "The angel said to me: 'These words are trustworthy and true; the Lord, the God of prophetic spirits, has sent his angel to show his servants what must happen very soon. Remember, I am coming soon! Happy the man who heeds the prophetic message of this book!" Saint Peter's second letter informs us: "In the Lord's eyes, one day is as a thousand years and a thousand years are as a day" (2 Peter 3:8). Here Christ says, "I am coming soon." He may be referring to eight billion years or so, while we are thinking about tomorrow morning at 10:12. God sees time differently than we do. "It is I, John, who heard and saw all these things, and when I heard and saw them I fell down to worship at the feet of the angel who showed them to me. But he said to me: 'No, get up! I am merely a fellow servant with you and your brothers the prophets and those who heed the message of this book. Worship God alone!' Then someone said to me: 'Do not seal up the prophetic words of this book, for the appointed time is near!' "

Earlier (in Chapter 1), I mentioned how my mother — as a young girl — asked a nun when the world would come to an end. And the nun answered, "When you die, and then you'll know." As a matter of fact, the nun's first answer to the question of the little girl standing before her was a little different: "In two seconds flat, if you don't sit down!" I imagine my mother was quite bewildered at this tart answer, but the nun softened and then said: "When you die, and then you'll know." Actually, both statements — "in about two seconds if you don't sit down" and "when you die" — are worth thinking about. Every moment is moving toward the end of this world for us, isn't it? No moment of the past will ever return.

So, these final words of Revelation are telling us here in today's world to *worship God alone*. We *must not seal up the prophetic words of this book;* we must proclaim this message everywhere because *the time is near.* Yes, Jesus has conquered and so will we if we continue to follow him. God has defeated Satan, but the devil can still tempt us. Therefore, we must be vigilant every moment.

Verses 11-15: "Let the wicked continue in their wicked ways, the depraved in their depravity! The virtuous must live on in their virtue and the holy ones in their holiness! Remember, I am coming soon! I bring with me the reward that will be given to each man as his conduct deserves. I am the Alpha and the Omega, the First and the Last, the Beginning and the End!" After this warning and exhortation, this passage concludes with a blessing for the faithful and a malediction for the unfaithful.

Verse 16: "It is I, Jesus, who have sent my angel to give you this testimony about the churches. I am the Root and Offspring of David, the Morning Star shining bright." I am the Messiah; I am the shining star that will lead you out of the darkness of sin and evil. Here, Jesus is also speaking to us: "I will lead you out of your darkest moments of despair and despondency when you are deeply depressed. I am the Morning Star shining in that darkness. Come to me, I will show you the way. Turn your life over to me."

Verse 17: Here "the Spirit and the Bride" invite all to "accept the gift of life-giving water." The Spirit represents the prophets of old. The Bride is the Church. God invites all to accept the life-giving waters (his grace). We may say yes or we may say no. We are free to do whatever we want to do. We may accept his "life-giving water" (his grace) or we may refuse it. God never forces us to love; he invites.

Verses 18,19: "I myself give witness to all who hear the prophetic words of this book. If anyone adds to these words, God will visit him with all the plagues described herein! If anyone takes from the words of this prophetic book, God will take away his share in the tree of life and the holy city described here!" This is a severe warning to anyone — including modern neoapocalyptic writers — not to tamper with what has been written in this Book.

Verses 20,21: "The One who gives this testimony says, 'Yes, I am coming soon!' Amen! Come, Lord Jesus! The grace of the Lord Jesus be with you all. Amen!"

"Come, Lord Jesus!" These words are extremely appropriate for the conclusion of the Book of Revelation. We have just made a profound meditation on the life of the Church. We have examined how it faced the existing problems in John's time, how the Lamb of God overcame the forces of evil, and how the faithful who follow the Lamb will be rewarded for their fidelity. God's Kingdom arrived at the First Coming of the Lord Jesus; its perfect fulfillment will arrive at his Second Coming. Christ is Victor! That is the message of Revelation. The entire Book reminds us of the poet's words: "Thou hast conquered, O pale Galilean!"

So each of us stands up and prays, "Come, Lord Jesus! Come, Lord, I'm ready!" This must be the basic stance we take in our personal lives. The Book of Revelation should guide us in everything we do. Christ's victory over Satan means that the devil cannot gain complete control. Evil still exists and we must face it. But we have God's promise that we will never be tempted beyond our strength. In time of temptation each person should ask himself or herself: "Whose name is on my forehead? With whose seal have I been marked?" Then each should pray, "Come, Lord Jesus!"

If we pray in this way, we begin to feel the inner peace that results from our abandonment of self to the Lord. Then we know that the Book of Revelation has revealed to us the message of life!

Review and Discussion

1. In Eden there was only one "tree of life." Why are there countless "trees of life" in the new Jerusalem?

2. How do we interpret the words in verse 7: "I am coming soon"?

3. What message does verse 8 contain for us?

4. What is the meaning of the words, "I am the Root and Offspring of David"?

5. What does the "Morning Star" symbolize?

6. In verse 17, the Old Testament prophets are symbolized by the _____ and the New Testament Church is called the _____ .

7. What does the term "life-giving waters" signify?

8. Is there a warning to modern interpreters to be found in verses 18 and 19?

9. To summarize the entire message of Revelation, fill in the following blanks:

    _____ has won. _____ still exists, but it can never _____ . The _____ is the bride of _____ . Those who follow the Lamb are numbered among the _____ . At the end of time evil forces will be hurled into the _____ and a new _____ will be created. Then all the faithful will be _____ . Each day we must depend upon the _____ of God to fight against the _____ of the world. Our daily prayer should be _____ .

10. How do you feel, personally, about the victory of Jesus depicted here in Revelation?
11. What do you do each day to show the Lord that you are freely accepting his ''living waters''?
12. Now that you have completed your study of Revelation, how have your ideas about it changed or grown?
13. What has meditating on this wonderful part of our Scriptures done for your personal life?

Moment of Prayerful Reflection

1. Read Revelation 22:17.
2. Meditate on your freedom as a son or daughter of God to follow or not to follow the Lord.

Let Us Pray

Lord Jesus, as we come to the end of this prayerful and reflective study of Revelation, we give you praise and glory for all the beautiful and powerful insights you have shared with us. Never again will we feel worried about the outcome of life, for we have seen revealed how you are victorious over any possible evil. Our hearts rest in confidence not only in your power but in your intimate love for each of us. May our days be spent in vigilance, overcoming evil where we can, with your powerful assistance, and waiting in love and peace for your coming. We lift our hearts to you this day and every day of our existence and sing songs of praise, adoration, honor, and glory. You are the Lord. . . . We are your people! Amen. Amen. Alleluia. Come, Lord Jesus. Amen. Alleluia!

OTHER BOOKS BY THE SAME AUTHOR

Discovering the Bible, Book One
Eight Simple Keys for Learning and Praying
Popular best seller explores eight themes and compares them as they appear first in the Old Testament and then in the New Testament. Themes presented are: Revelation, Covenant, Sin, Messiah, Election, Law, Redemption, Love.* **$3.95**

Discovering the Bible, Book Two
Eight Simple Keys for Learning and Praying
Continues the easy-to-follow approach of Book One, focusing on these themes: Community, Faith, Holiness, Suffering, Hospitality, Worship, Justice, Discipleship.* **$3.95**

*Each chapter includes background information, Scripture references, discussion questions, and prayer service.

OTHER SCRIPTURE HELPS FROM LIGUORI

You and the Bible
by Patrick Kaler, C.SS.R.
Written to help Catholics who may be confused or bewildered by the well-meaning but simplistic "interpretations" that are often presented as truth, this book provides information about the Bible that today's Catholics need to know and offers easy-to-understand answers. A basic Bible "survival kit" for today's Catholics. **$2.50**

150 Fun Facts Found in the Bible
Treat yourself to the kind of fascinating facts you can find when you wander through the pages of the Bible. Fill your day with fun facts; fill your head with inspiring ideas; fill your life with marvels and miracles, smiles and surprises. **$5.95**

Order from your local bookstore or write to:
Liguori Publications, Box 060, Liguori, MO 63057-9999
(Please add $1.00 for postage and handling for orders under $5.00; $1.50 for orders over $5.00.)